Praise for **NO TOURISTS ALLOWED** by Shannon Egan

"As with all the very best memoirs, it's what Shannon Egan has to say about common truth and hidden secrets that resonates the most. Shannon's journey is a gripping story about love-of-self, loss-of-self, ambition, failure, religious indoctrination and escaping the mental chains that hold us as people, us as tribes, and us as nations captive. Shannon's writing is fast-paced, vivid, and absolutely rooted in self-discovery. *No Tourists Allowed* should be required reading for every addict who has spent a lifetime fighting their demons through the foggy lens of religious indoctrination."

Brian Lee Durfee, author of *The Forgetting Moon*
Simon & Schuster 2016

# No Tourists
# ALLOWED

Seeking Inner Peace and Sobriety in War-Torn Sudan

SHANNON EGAN

Shannon Egan is an international journalist, author, and advocate for addiction recovery.

For information:
www.ShannonEgan.com

ShannonMaeEgan@gmail.com

Author's Note: Most of the events described happened as related; a few were expanded. Some of the individuals portrayed are composites of more than one person, and most names of individuals have been changed. The conversations in the book all come from the author's recollections, though they are not written to represent word-for-word transcripts. Rather, the author has retold them in a way that evokes the feeling and meaning of what was said. In all instances, the essence of events and dialogue are accurate. Although the author has made every effort to ensure that the information in this book was correct at press time, the author will not assume and hereby disclaim any liability to any party for any loss, damage, or disruption caused by errors or omissions, whether such errors or omissions result from negligence, accident, or any other cause.

Egan, Shannon.

    NO TOURISTS ALLOWED / Shannon Egan.

    ISBN-13: 978-0-692-43625-7

# Contents

# Dedication

This book is dedicated to the person struggling
with drug or alcohol addiction.

I hope that by reading about my struggles,
you will find purpose and meaning in your own
and know for yourself that
recovery is possible.

To my dad and mom for your wisdom, love,
and support—always.

And especially to my brave and spirited
Sudanese friends.

*Namaste.*

# Chapter 1

At six, I'm a sensitive girl. I play in the dirt to get a whiff of the earth and keep watch over all of my friends scurrying about: the worm, the katydid, the praying mantis, and yes, even the (not so terrifying) spider. I want to protect them, the tiny and vulnerable, these bugs that are not unlike me in my world of God-fearing adults and Mormon temples of Salt Lake City, Utah. In the bugs' world I am strong: I crush one ant, accidentally. I shield another from harm by moving it to the grass. Here, I am the harm and the second chance.

I'm not sure how or why, but I have this feeling that every bug, no matter how weird-looking or irrelevant it may seem, is important. It has a big, beautiful purpose, which again, I don't really comprehend, because I'm just a kid, but still it's something I *feel* and *strongly* in my little kid gut. Why else would a bug exist and with such awesome characteristics? An ant can carry up to fifty times its own weight—on its mandibles! Ants were the first farmers—and lived alongside the dinosaurs! All this staying power and talent means the only thing keeping the ant from outlasting and outplaying us all is its *size*.

I can relate. I can't protect myself from being squashed by those that loom above me on a daily basis: the all-powerful adults. I wonder—if I were just a little bit bigger would they be able to see that I, too, have a purpose? Right now it's hidden in my tiny frame, but it's *there*. If only they could feel it the way I feel the ants' purpose, maybe I'd be more relevant in their eyes and they wouldn't be so quick to shoo me away.

This is the wish I offer up to the universe whenever I get the chance. Shooting star or dandelion—my wish is the same.

That and I wish for my very own carton of mint chocolate chip ice cream so I can eat straight out of the box whenever I want, just like my mom. Neither wish comes true, at least not in the timeframe I want them too, and that's hard on me because I don't understand why I'm treated like I'm a *Latrodectus mactans* (black widow spider) or a *Loxosceles reclusa* (brown recluse). Am I hideous? Annoying? A dangerous pest?

We live in a small, brick rambler in Salt Lake County, where over half of the population is indoctrinated into the Church of Jesus Christ of Latter-day Saints. Specifically, over 500,000 members, four temples, six missions, 174 stakes, the Tabernacle Choir, the Prophet of God, and most of his twelve apostles—all packed into 740 square miles. This makes Utah the only state with a Mormon majority, and the only state with a majority population belonging to a single church.

Utah is beautifully scenic, a playground for outdoor enthusiasts. We have national parks (Zion and Bryce Canyon) and a handful of ski resorts, and on our state license plates are the words *Greatest Snow on Earth*. My brothers and sisters—there are six of us—grow up skiing and snowboarding at Brighton ski resort on Wednesday evenings because it is the closest one to home and we can get a buddy pass at Arctic Circle, which allows us to bring our friends. These outings are some of my favorite times with my family. But as in all families, there are other times that are painful, and we don't talk about them because our parents would kill us, and what would we say? It's extremely important in our neighborhood and church ward to pretend we are the perfect Mormon family that reads scriptures every night, has "home evening" once a week, and pays tithing regularly. We do all these things, but our family is far from perfect.

My mom likes to hit us and *hard*. Once when I was really little, maybe four, she dragged me down the hallway by my hair, and I still can't forget the way my head stung for days afterwards. Every day that my dad is at work my mom goes into a rage, and sometimes I hide in my bedroom closet or below the deck in our backyard so she can't find me. I'm there with my bug buddies, so I don't mind. Not a day goes by when dad's gone that she isn't screaming at the top of her lungs because somebody didn't clean the toilet correctly or forgot to pick up their socks. I'm scared of her and when I tell my dad, he shushes me.

"I want peace, not justice, okay?" he says.

I don't know what this means but I nod my head and smile. He seems powerless to protect me from mom, and I'm not sure why. Maybe he doesn't stand up for me because it's somehow my fault; I'm deserving of the screams and the blows. I vow to be better and start to write her love letters, which I deliver on the days she's really pissed. I slide them under her bedroom door while she naps. But the letters only make her angrier. She says I'm trying to manipulate her, and because she's older and wiser, I wonder if she is right. Maybe I'm just bad all around and nothing I do will ever make up for it.

Dad works a lot of overtime at Kennecott Copper Mine so we can pay the bills and afford to go school shopping at Deseret Industries. He's hardly ever home, but when he is, he hides behind the newspaper asking for "a little peace and quiet" so he can read Calvin and Hobbes in his tattered Brigham Young University sweatshirt. All the kids love it when dad is home because mom is more subdued around him and dad is gentler with us, so we *all* get a little peace and quiet. I'm not really sensitive to his stress because I don't work sixty-five hours per week, so when he gets home I bombard him with questions.

"Dad, are there any other gods beside the Mormon God? Do you know what God the ladybug prays to? Why do you think God made the ladybug or the daddy long leg? Do they have bug churches underground like we do?"

"Shannon, knock it off. Of course there's only one God. Now go play with your sisters."

His response cuts me, but I pretend I'm okay. I will have to find somebody else to ask my questions to because there are so many things I've been learning in church that I don't understand. For instance: if I'm as bad as mom says, will I go to spirit prison? When I'm sixteen will I have to do baptisms for the dead in the temple like everyone else? The idea of being baptized for a dead person really creeps me out, so I take my questions to anyone who will listen: my primary teacher, my friends, my sisters and brothers. The response is always the same: don't ask stupid questions, don't be ridiculous, stop doubting in God and his teachings.

When I'm eight, my dad baptizes me. I wear a white jumpsuit and he holds me under so that every inch of my body is submerged. Total submersion is key in a Mormon baptism. It's the only way to truly be cleansed of all your sins. I don't think I have committed many. I hit my sisters sometimes, I don't clean my room, and I once stole a piece of caramel taffy from the grocery store. But I'm a good kid overall. The problem is that I'm a good kid who doesn't really want to be baptized. I say this out loud and my mom tells me that my constant questioning and doubting are acts of sin. I don't know if I doubt anything—I just feel curious—but according to her, it means I have a rebellious spirit.

"Shannon, I'm concerned about you. I think the Devil has a strong hold over your spirit. You need to take your baptism and confirmation very seriously. If you don't listen to the promptings of the Holy Ghost you may end up down a dark path one day."

I imagine the Devil gripping my spirit with evil red hands and I shiver. Maybe it will be good for me to be baptized and confirmed after all, so I can receive the gift of the Holy Ghost, a supernatural companion who will be with me at all times in order to keep me on God's straight and narrow path. I don't tell my mom that the Holy Ghost freaks me out or that I don't particularly want to walk in a straight line for the rest of my life. Whenever we've gone hiking as a family, I've always enjoyed the curvy trails. How boring will my life be without a bend or even a scary drop-off that gets my blood pumping and my heart racing?

Despite my hesitations, I go through it with a big smile plastered over my face. This is sure to make my parents proud. I tell myself this is for the best and shove down the fears that are trying to crawl up my throat and out of my mouth. The fears want to be heard: I'm terrified of what will happen if I don't abide by the rules and commit to these beliefs. I certainly don't want to be grounded or have my mouth washed out with soap, and I hate being called *bad* in front of my brothers and sisters.

I try to fit in but it's too late. I'm contaminated. Evil might really have a strong grip on my heart and I'll have to keep a close eye on myself because not even *I* am aware of my own manipulations.

At eight I already feel like an outlaw, and every outlaw, even an eight-year-old one, needs a place of refuge. I set up my camp in a dirt field behind our house, armed with a notepad and a pencil so I can document important things like my bug buddies. Knowledge is power and I want a lot of it, so one day, I can be powerful too. I spend my free time hunkered down, taking notes.

*Today there are four potato bugs under the big rock next to the Ferrins' shed. Three are bundled up and taking a nap, and one is moving about. I wonder what they've been up to all day,* I write.

Silly notes, but I like to write because it helps me understand the world around me. In my imagination, I'm a detective and I'm trying to figure out how we're all connected. The clues are everywhere because everything matters, even the crumble of dirt on my sneakers. Nature is a treasure trove and everything in it glistens like jewels.

In the summertime, I sprawl out on the soft dirt of my refuge and look up into the pretty blue sky to enjoy the fluffy white clouds. They remind me of giant puffed marshmallows and make my stomach growl. The birds chirp as they whiz by and I squint to see past them in hopes of catching a glimpse of God. He lives up there in Heaven with His angels who praise Him day and night, as I've been told. I don't know if God is a male or why anybody would want to make their entire existence about the worship of another—but I do know that here in this field God likes who I am, just as I am, and that I have a purpose, and one day it will become apparent to me, and that I needn't worry about it.

Here I'm safe to believe in anything and do anything— even to wonder aloud. So I talk to God, not on my knees with a scripted prayer like we do as a family, but in my own words. I lay back with my arms folded under my head for a cushion, and I giggle a lot because it feels kind of dorky. I wonder what people will think if they find me here chuckling at the sky like a crazy person. They might think I've gone mad, like the Hatter in Wonderland, and this thought makes me giggle even harder. I swear I can feel God laughing with me and it warms my heart right up—like when we have a hot cocoa after a day of sledding. I decide to make another wish, not on a dandelion or shooting star, but on a little bird happening by.

"I wish I could freeze time and stay here forever."

I know God hears me and understands. Under this pretty summer sky with the marshmallow clouds that make my stomach growl, God and I are great friends.

\* \* \*

Time didn't freeze. By the age of fourteen, that God—my sweet, tender comrade—was dead.

He got pulverized into bite-sized pieces and then hurled into oblivion by everyone who knew better than me. A new God emerged, one that demanded I look, think, and act like everybody else. The thing was, all the girls I knew wanted to wear garments, have babies, and take care of their husbands. (A terrible cliché, but one that does exist in Utah.) Me? I wanted to travel the world. I'd give anything to be the captain of a pirate ship with a shiny hook for a hand. In my dreams, I'd sail into the ocean with a school of whales following my lead. In real life, I wanted to travel to Africa so I could dodge snakes in remote jungles and chase bad guys like Indiana Jones. I liked how Indy was sometimes afraid to take a situation on but did it anyway, and he was a true explorer. He also had a purpose, which was to save people who could not save themselves.

"Shannon, this is never going to happen. Let go of the dream," my parents told me. They expected me to marry a nice missionary boy, settle down, and multiply and replenish the Earth. I never thought of babies or marriage. These ideas were completely uninteresting to me.

At fifteen, things started to get ugly. My dirt field had become a hostile, contentious environment, no longer lovely or enchanted. I had to boycott it altogether because it brought out an insatiable thirst for adventure, which was starting to get me into serious trouble. People thought I was foolish because I didn't want to do what everyone else was doing, and I could hardly stand the looks of contempt in their eyes. My options were pretty clear: obey and honor the rules of my community—which meant going to church and reading scriptures—or spend my teenage years grounded and emotionally chained up in a shame that was quickly consuming my mind like black tar devours a flower garden.

I tried living according to their standards and I'd give anything to blend in but it was never good enough. To them, I was the "black sheep" in need of saving. I began to wonder more and more…maybe I was crazy? Maybe the devil was really inside me and everyone around me was right. Maybe I was headed for spirit prison or worse: hell. I was humiliated repeatedly and felt myself starting to shut down. I stopped being able to tell the difference between my actions and my true self: was I doing bad things or was *I* just bad? Eventually these thoughts gained enough momentum that I could no longer control them. They took on a monster-like persona with sharp teeth and a vicious bite and followed me everywhere, even in my dreams.

"You're a devil," they barked at me. "You can't be trusted and must rot in hell!"

What had I done wrong? It was as if I'd been convicted of murder, regardless of not actually having killed anyone, and there was not a drop of forgiveness in sight. When I'd wake up in a panic, I could vaguely hear God, my old confidante, whispering to me, "Be strong! Know these monsters are mistaken and their words are a result of their own fears. *It is not about you. You are always worthy.*"

This voice was distant, drowned out by a thousand thunderstorms, and yet it gave me the courage to stand up and fight. I was bigger now and could take them, I was sure of it. I used my imagination to transform into a Fearless Warrior Princess on an important mission. I would fight for the kids who were bullied by religious dogma, hurt by their parents, and had no voice in a dark, confused world, and I would not give up until we were heard! I wore an invisible chest plate, which would protect my heart and was encrusted with rubies, my birthstone and lucky charm. In my hand, I held up a long, silver sword so I could feel tall and brave—just as I did when I was six, with the ants.

"I am free and have the right to choose who I will be and what I will believe in!" I proclaimed.

This horrified my parents. "Shame on you! Why can't you be like everyone else?"

"Why can't you see that who I am is enough?"

My parents didn't know what to do with me, so they grounded me for months at a time. I refused to be punished for simply speaking my truth, but the only thing I could think to do to protect myself was run away. If they found me, I'd run again, seeking shelter anywhere, including a shack off the Bangerter Highway close to home. There I made friends with mice and slept on a mud floor until they found me again. I wish they could've understood this was not about being rebellious or defiant, but about protecting my basic human right: *freedom of expression*. It would've saved us a lot of pain and heartache, but instead, we battled it out for years.

I also wish I could say I triumphed, not just for myself, but for all the imaginary people I was fighting for back then. I thought I was Indy and could save them without realizing how impossible it is to be a champion when you need a champion. In the end, the monsters won and I too hated myself for not being like everyone else.

Why did I have to be born so devilish and defiant, the black sheep of the family?

***

Lush. Drunk. Stoner. By eighteen, these were my new labels. The moment I was legal, I moved out of my parents' house and into a two-bedroom apartment with Jessica, a party girl I'd met through a mutual friend. She was a total snob with long lustrous hair and all the best clothing brands, but I wanted to get out of my house and she was in need of a roommate. We got jobs together at Garth Sports near Vine Street in Murray. And I never had to go to another church outing again.

Jessica and I walked to work, just two minutes away, and then hurried home after our shift so we could smoke pot and play Pandemonium on the PlayStation with our friends. We'd make tacos layered with mashed potatoes, tomato sauce, and cheese, and devour them like they were everything. What did we care? As Pink Floyd put it: we were only coming through in waves, a fleet of ships smoking on the horizon, receding from our pain and comfortably numb.

After a year of daily pot smoking, I was a mindless robot. But I didn't realize it until one day when I missed work. I forgot I was on the schedule and realized my mistake the following morning. Before my next shift, I thought up a perfectly dramatic excuse to keep from getting fired and went straight to my boss to share it.

"Hey Dave, can I talk to you for a minute?"

Dave was busy doing paperwork in his office. He looked up, but only briefly.

"Hello, what's up?"

"Um…so, about yesterday. Look, I'm really sorry I didn't show up. I know it was really irresponsible of me, but my sister was in a car accident and I had to go to the hospital and make sure she was okay and I was so freaked out and worried about her that I completely forgot to check in. Again, I'm so sorry. It won't happen again."

I had Dave's attention now. He was staring at me with the strangest expression on his face, so strange, in fact, that it made me squirm nervously in the doorway. *He's going to fire me, right here, right now.*

"Shannon, you were *here yesterday.*"

It was my turn to stare at him mystified. When what he said finally hit home (it took a minute because my brain worked in slow-motion those days) I laughed the whole thing off like it was some big joke.

*Haha, Dave! Of course I know I was here yesterday! That would be totally nuts to forget something like that, right? What a funny joke!*

In order to suppress this awful event, I went home during lunch and lit a joint. I was hoping the weed would help make light of the situation, but it didn't. Instead, while high, it replayed over and over again in my head. It started to really bug me that I couldn't remember an entire day of my life. How many other days had I blacked out? Is this how I wanted to live?

And really, what was so funny about an eighteen-year-old girl frying her brain because she *hated who she was?*

My childhood monsters still had their grip on me and the weed was like a tranquilizer, knocking those bastards out with one hit. It was, so far, the only thing I'd come across that was strong enough to shut them up. However, after the Garth Sports incident, I switched up my numbing technique from heavy drug use to heavy alcohol use with a dash of pot, mushrooms, ketamine, cocaine—whatever I could get my hands on.

But my true love was vodka, straight up and warm—it burned so good. I loved her, I hated her, my precious Vodka. She could magically transform me into a powerful seductress, the kind that dances on tables and everybody fawns over. Since I was a pretty brunette with luscious hourglass curves and those sexy bedroom eyes that few men can resist, the attention was easy to garner. That was, until I took one too many shots and then, well, I'd turn dark and become a woman possessed by rage. I'd hit, slap, bite. Some of the guys even liked this, but that wasn't the point. Eventually, I'd lose all my fans and find myself alone. Which was okay with me. I said it was all a bunch of bull anyway.

One night when I was intoxicated, I stumbled over to our apartment pool while everyone was upstairs partying. The moon was out, splashing yellow onto the smooth, watery surface. I peered over the side and a face jumped out at me like a ghost, haunted. It was the Fearless Warrior Princess from my childhood, but she looked broken and lost—not very warrior-like at all— and she was singing one of our favorite tunes, "Fast Car" by Tracey Chapman:

*I want a ticket to anywhere*
*Maybe we make a deal*
*Maybe together we can get somewhere*
*Any place is better…*

Seeing the Warrior again after so many years was disconcerting. I didn't want her to witness me like this, drunk and stupid. So I ignored her and gave way to my rage. Anger was stronger than shame and could crush humiliation in a matter of seconds. Charged by the alcohol, my pain, and the moon, I ran up a flight of stairs and pounded my fist into a glass panel protecting a fire hydrant. I struck it with all my might. After five or so hard thrusts, blood finally burst from my right knuckle in a hot, oozing stream. For a moment, relief washed over me. I breathed. And then finally, after what felt like an eternity, tears flowed.

I'd dreamt one night that my childhood monsters had strapped me to a metal chair and carved out my tear ducts with a dull knife. This was becoming a recurring dream of mine. I knew what it meant. The monsters wanted me to know that it didn't matter how *I* felt, it only mattered how *they* felt. I was irrelevant in their world and if I couldn't cry, I couldn't acknowledge what had been done to me. Nor could I acknowledge my own heartache.

I stumbled back to the poolside and wept as blood dripped onto the face of my inner champion, giving her an eerie crimson glow. I stared at my reflection behind layers of detachment, a shield for my shame. It hurt to see myself so lost and wounded. Once upon a time, I believed I was good, even *born for something great*. Where did my convictions go? And how did I get them back?

My warrior, still singing our Tracey Chapman song, responded with:

*You gotta make a decision*
*Leave tonight or live and die this way*

She was right. Addiction would one day nearly kill me, but that was not this day. On this day, I very much wanted to live and "get somewhere," but I didn't know where that somewhere was or how I was going to get there as a drunk.

***

At twenty-two, I got my wild ways under enough control to enroll in Salt Lake Community College (SLCC). I decided I was going to be a psychologist so I could develop the skills needed to dig deep and figure out what had happened to me. I began to form professional questions in response to my raw experiences: Why couldn't I form attachments to people or material things? Why couldn't I cry? I'd started having panic attacks and simple breathing was becoming difficult. In a few years, I'd be diagnosed with asthma.

I'd been learning about the term *psychosomatic* and the effects of childhood abuse (physical, mental, and emotional) on the adult body and how emotional traumas, suppressed humiliations, and stored-up rage can manifest themselves as serious adult health problems such as depression, anorexia, cancer, and *addiction*. Is this what was happening to me? And if

I could work through my traumas, would the panic attacks stop? Could I one day breathe without struggle?

I felt guilty for trying to link my current dysfunctional state to my childhood experiences but I couldn't shake the feeling that they were strongly connected to my adult feelings of powerlessness and diminished human dignity. Luckily, I stumbled across the work of Alice Miller, a Ph.D. in philosophy, psychology, and sociology, as well as a researcher on childhood and the author of thirteen books. Miller's work suggested my guilt was directly related to worldwide social norms that *require* a child to respect and obey her parents. This is even mandated in the Fourth Commandment: *honor thy father and thy mother.*

Like the concepts of spirit prison and baptisms for the dead, this commandment haunted me. Was it suggesting that no matter *what* my parents did or believed in I had to accept their beliefs at face value? What if their actions or beliefs hurt me? Where were the rights of the child or the commandment stating that it was a parent's duty to protect, nurture, and respect their child's individuality—even if their child wanted to establish a relationship with God that was different from their own?

These were radical concepts for a Mormon community knee deep in the Ten Commandments. But I expressed them anyways. The guilt being heaped upon me by those older and wiser resembled another term I'd been learning about: *emotional blackmail.* This term referred to using fear, obligation, or guilt to control someone's behavior. Emotional blackmail included threatening and/or punishing an individual—directly or indirectly—in order to get a desired behavioral outcome. This method may have been effective in getting me to conform momentarily, but the long-term effects were what led to, according to Alice Miller, psychosomatic symptoms, and these symptoms had negative consequences not only on individuals but on whole societies. Miller believed that the lack of protection for children and their rights was society's ultimate betrayal and that it was time for traditional methods of child rearing to be dramatically overhauled.

I had developed an interest in psychology when I was fifteen and my parents had taken me to a therapist for having sex with my boyfriend. The situation wasn't particularly pleasant because my parents went with me and the therapist was Mormon. When I recall the memory of our first session together it's always through a fisheye lens in my brain giving it a highly curved and distorted focus. We were sitting on hard, wooden chairs across from the psychologist, Dr. Brownstone, who was sitting comfortably on a beige couch diagonally from us. There was very little space between any of the furniture, which meant we were all a little too close for comfort.

"We found a letter from her boyfriend and it indicated the two of them had sex. He's eighteen and should know better. We've contacted his parents to let them know that we're pressing charges for statutory rape," my mom explained.

Dr. Brownstone tsked-tsked and then turned toward me with an exaggerated look of concern. He was bone-thin and balding with a gray patch of hair on the lower half of his head just like Mr. Burns from the Simpsons. His creepy mannerisms also matched the cartoon character, and I wanted to punch him.

"Tell me, Shannon why'd you engage in sex with this man? Do you love him? Was it for pleasure? Did you orgasm?"

I was fifteen and dying of embarrassment. Hot red surfaced on my cheeks and then shot like a skyrocket to my ears. I fidgeted in my chair while Dr. Burns—I mean, Dr. Brownstone watched me like a hawk. I looked to my parents for guidance on what to say and who to be. There was no way I was going to be honest about anything, not if I wanted to live. The vibe in that room was all about control, dominance, and fear—not understanding or love or connection.

"You see, I highly doubt you had an orgasm. Few women, let alone underage girls, *do* during sex. So if it wasn't for pleasure, what was it for?" Dr. Brownstone said.

"Well, Shannon? What do you have to say for yourself?" my mom said.

"No, I didn't have an orgasm," I said.

I started to cry and the conversations stopped. They seemed satisfied by my tears, perhaps taking them as a sign of regret and remorse, but really I was crying because I felt very much like Frankenstein's monster: rejected, neglected, and bullied by my own creators. They had no problems showing their disgust for me in front of a stranger. Why would they? The stranger just validated their belief that I was worse than an eight-foot-tall monster with translucent yellow skin. I was a Mormon girl who had premarital sex.

As harsh as this experience was, I was intrigued by the profession and knew therapy should be better, and so, in college, I sought therapy once again, this time on my terms. My new therapist, Dr. Reynolds, was a jolly soul and actually resembled Santa with a big gut, white beard, and a balding head. He'd always greet me with a side hug, which at first I thought was weird, but after a while I really looked forward to those side hugs. In our sessions, Dr. Reynolds tried to connect me with my inner child, but the poor girl was terribly jaded and resistant. Sometimes his methods worked, sometimes they didn't, but overall, I always benefited from our chats. He never invalidated my experience and that meant everything to me.

Dr. Reynolds also helped me to recognize some of my unhealthy thought patterns, like my habit of thinking in terms of all or nothing. He pointed out that I probably thought in these terms because extremes were all I'd ever known. In Utah, you either had a one-way ticket to heaven or hell.

"Perhaps," he said, "you'd benefit from a little gray in your life."

I laughed at that. "Easier said than done, Reynolds!"

"Shannon, this is not a laughing matter."

Dr. Reynolds was onto my tricks. He knew I used humor and laughter as a way of deflecting pain, and he didn't let me get away with it.

"Look, you can't sit here and wallow in the pain of your childhood forever, blaming your parents, the Mormons, or anyone else. Today you're an adult. This means *you* are in charge of *you* and it's time for *you* to begin the process of rewiring your brain so that it becomes a tool for peace and love in your life."

"But how do I do that when I don't know what's true about God and what isn't?"

"Wounds heal with love, Shannon. Learn to love yourself and others, and the truth about God, the universe, and your purpose will sort itself out."

Had I stuck with school, I might've become a really wise psychologist like Dr. Reynolds, but I will never know. My love for freedom, change, and travel outweighed my love for classrooms, textbooks, and lectures. Travel in particular had this strong magnetic hold on me and I couldn't pull away. It would suck me into a daydream in the middle of class or study hour, which I preferred. Eventually I discovered a Learning Service group at SLCC where students traveled throughout the U.S. to learn about culture and be of service. I had heard it was a very hard group to get into, but a great way to get school credit and live out my dream, so I applied. After a really tough interview in front of a handful of my peers, I was accepted, and over the course of the year we raised money for trips to NYC and Hawaii. I discovered a lot of first loves on those trips: flying high in airplanes among the clouds and the birds, snorkeling and swimming alongside the sea turtles in Hawaii, and in NYC, a deep appreciation for chaos and the seedy underworld of the subway.

It occurred to me that the people in my life thought I was just saying I wanted to travel so that I could be "different." They thought I was just causing trouble. It made sense that this was their conclusion, for when only heaven and hell are offered as options, anybody who is not on the side of the saints must be a sinner. The good thing: Dr. Reynolds was right about the truth and lies, and sorting things out in time. The bad thing? These things would unravel very slowly. And in the meantime, my self-perception was completely distorted. It was as if I were looking at myself through that same fisheye lens. It magnified my flaws up front and squished any good traits I had into the margins. This made life painful and I started drinking again. At twenty-one, I found myself in handcuffs for driving under the influence.

It was my first official arrest but not my last.

# Chapter 2

*A* few months before my twenty-fourth birthday, Artemis, the Greek goddess of the wilderness and the hunt, shot an arrow at my head and yelled, *Brace yourself, bitch! We're going on an adventure!*

The Artemis of legend roams mountains and forests with her nymphs in tow while hunting panthers, hinds, and stags. She remains completely unattached, preferring to live alone rather than marry or have children. I imagine she was beautiful, feisty, and ruthless, which is why she shot an arrow at me. She wanted my attention, dammit! Artemis is my goddess archetype, a female powerhouse I consider kindred the way Anne of Green Gables and her friend Diana are kindred—except Artemis and I wouldn't be "bosom buddies" creating blissful memories the way best friends do. No, Artemis was present that morning to entice me to do as she did and venture out into the wild *alone*. I already knew in the depths of my soul what the adventure must entail: uncivilized territory, wildlife, and a test of survival.

Then I remembered my childhood dream: *Africa*.

The timing of Artemis' arrow was perfect. I had not only graduated from SLCC with an associate degree in behavioral science, but had done so with high honors, which had really lifted my self-esteem. Plus, I'd gone on a few trips into Utah's mountains with just a backpack and the crumble of dirt on my sneakers. At first, traveling solo was a terrifying ordeal. Everyone told me I'd get raped or attacked by a moose. (By the way, I did come across a moose once and all we did was stare at each other peacefully and then go on our merry ways). But before my first trip, I'd gone to REI to pick up some camping essentials. When I ran into a saleswoman there with flowing silvery hair and sun-cracked lips, I told her about my plans in hopes that she would be able to provide me with some unbiased advice.

"Do you think it's irresponsible of me to go camping alone… as a woman?"

The saleswoman looked at me straight in the eyes and with great conviction said, "Trust in the universe."

If she'd said "trust in God" I may have zapped her with my imaginary Taser, but she didn't. The word *universe* reverberated within me because it suggested a higher power and purpose that wasn't tainted with guilt, manipulation, and control. These four words were exactly what I needed to hear to be able to harness the courage required of someone willing to seek out their own path.

Through my solo trips and school I began to establish some balance and make sense of the world, despite remaining stuck between extremes: I was either a full-blown lush or die-hard churchgoer, and the cycle was vicious. I'd drink to escape the guilt of not fitting in with my community until I'd feel so guilty for drinking I'd have to quit cold turkey. The bouts of sobriety would last two to six months until the guilt from all my past sins would become too much to bear, sending me right back where I started: madly in love with that other great goddess I adored and revered, Vodka.

I almost wrote an ode to Vodka and included it here. My ego really wants to get across how good I became at being that darling, drunk seductress. But why would I want to glorify a habit that eventually led to multiple DUIs, a car crash, jail time, sixty days on an ankle monitor, and four years of court-ordered probation? I drank because I *hurt,* and there was nothing glamorous about that.

Yet if it weren't for the shame, guilt, and consequences of drinking, I might've stayed drunk forever because *rock n' roll* fit my rambunctious spirit way more than that copycat box I felt the Mormons were trying to cram me into. This left me teetering between a drink and the scriptures all day, every day. It was my silent, secret struggle.

My dad was always quoting Alma, a prophet in the Book of Mormon. One day, I thought that perhaps it was time to consider the point they were both trying to make. The prophet says, "And now, my son, all men that are in a state of nature, or I would say in a carnal state, are in the gall of bitterness and in the bonds of iniquity; they are without God in the world, and they have gone contrary to the nature of God; therefore, they are in a state contrary to the nature of happiness."

My dad was hinting that I'd become an unhappy, bitter woman without God, and if I just stopped my wicked ways and committed to absolutely *everything* the church had asked of me, this guilt would subside and things would fall into place. At this point, I was tired of the good girl/bad girl dance. I wanted it to stop. (Even when I was acting as a devout church member, I'd allow myself the occasional slip up. Translation: daily masturbation and a sip or two of Coca-Cola). I'd never gone all-in before, which was no doubt why God was so angry with me and why I always failed at the church thing. This was my time to surrender and become the ultimate Mormon, a "Molly Mormon," which is what the Mormons called the girls that didn't let a guy get to first base and made Relief Society and the Singles Ward a top priority.

This was it. I would finally be *happy*.

A proper Molly Mormon has regular meetings with her bishop and mine was called Bishop Smith. He was a serious but soft-spoken man and I felt comfortable enough to be honest with him about my struggles.

"Shannon, if you really want this, you'll need to start the repentance process now and make some goals. Write this down. I'd like you to consider serving a small church calling at some point and get a calendar if you don't already have one. Document the days you pray and participate in daily scripture study. This will help you visualize your progress. I don't want you being too hard on yourself throughout this process or it won't work."

I took notes and assured him I was super serious and would do everything he recommended.

"That's good. But there's no fast track to forgiveness and this process could take up to a year. And, quite frankly, I'm really concerned about your drinking. Will you have withdrawals? Do you need treatment?"

I told him I'd gone for months at a time without alcohol and never experienced withdrawals—only an increase in depression, anxiety, and panic attacks. He suggested therapy and medication, and then he had a light bulb moment.

"Have you considered serving a mission? I know you're not interested in marrying right away and we could use more women in the field. Plus, you'd get to travel."

Mormon missionaries are volunteer representatives of the LDS Church who participate in proselytizing, church service, humanitarian aid, and community service. Missions typically last two years for males, eighteen months for females and older couples, and a missionary may be called to serve in any one of the church's 405 missions worldwide.

This sounded like the perfect way for me to live out my dreams, even as a Molly Mormon.

"Okay, how about we make that your big goal to shoot for. Let's say, in one year, you'll plan to take out your endowments. Sound good?"

Taking out one's "endowments" is an important step as a Mormon and a mandatory one in order to serve a mission or get married. It happens in a temple ceremony designed to prepare participants to become kings, queens, priests, and priestesses in the afterlife. When they receive their temple garments, they're expected to wear them every day and night for the rest of their lives.

Wow, I thought. This is my big payoff?

It hardly felt like a reward, but it's what a Molly Mormon would want.

The year went by slowly. What I found most interesting about the whole process was that giving up masturbation was a lot harder than giving up alcohol. At the end of my journey, I went to see Bishop Smith.

"I'm so proud of you. You worked very hard for this. I can schedule an appointment for you to attend the temple next week if you want?"

I nodded and smiled, but something felt off. I didn't feel at all the way I'd expected to feel after finally giving in and surrendering my ego to God, along with an entire year of my life. I mean, being righteous was a seriously tough job, and I'd put blood, sweat, and tears into trying. So why didn't I feel happy like the scriptures had promised? All I felt was empty, confused, and a little annoyed. As I walked out of Bishop Smith's office, I realized I was more than just a little annoyed—I was seething like Dante's inferno.

I sat in my red Chevy Cavalier in the parking lot, staring at the church. The building was an exact replica of all the other Mormon churches around town: brick, brown, boring. Inside, the layout was the same. The drinking fountains were always next to the bathroom, which were next to the foyer or the nursery, which were next to the gym and blah, blah, blah, everything a copy of another, like the missionaries and their haircuts and the girls with their dreams of homemaking.

*Me? A missionary? Is this really what I want?*

No! I didn't! Nor did I particularly enjoy the last year. I had never liked the idea of having everything figured out and decided upon. I wanted the experience of seeking and finding and knowing for myself. I wanted to be able to ask questions and get to the heart of matters without being shamed for it.

Suddenly it dawned on me that although I hadn't obtained the ever-elusive state of happiness that I'd originally planned for, I'd actually gained something better. Something less fleeting and more consistent than happiness. I'd gained clarity. I could finally say, after all these years, I'd given this church, which had dominated my life, my entire life, everything I had, and that in the end it didn't really work for me.

And that was okay.

The church clearly worked for a lot of people, such as my older sister Holly, whom I adore and trust, and that was okay too. The experience had ultimately brought clarity about who I wasn't, which helped magnify who I *was*, or at least who I wanted to be, which was still kind of blurry. Nevertheless, I could finally begin my quest for purpose without the chains of this religion holding me back.

*Who am I? What do I believe in? Where do I fit in?* I could hardly wait to find out.

For the first time in my life, I left the church parking lot beaming.

\*\*\*

Artemis shot her arrow just a couple months after this pivotal moment. The timing was perfect and I had my sights set on Africa.

I sold my car and packed my bags. All I needed was a destination and a plan. Some people might get overwhelmed by the idea of picking a random country and moving there, alone, without any money or a passport, but for me, it was like a puzzle without any missing pieces, and all I had to do was relax and let it sort itself out.

So that's what I did. I figured I wasn't the first lone adventurer in the world attempting to travel without any money or a plan. And I was right. As soon as I typed *travel the world for free* into Google, hundreds of options popped up. Everything I needed to know was there in links, books, and blogs. The internet turned a seemingly impossible task into one with endless possibilities. After a week, I discovered an e-book that would turn my dream into a reality. This book provided an extensive list of locations around the world that allowed travelers to clean for a warm bed or cook for a hearty meal. My major barrier was that I had very little money for a plane ticket. Luckily, the e-book had a solution for that too. It recommended teaching abroad, since most schools would pay for room, travel, and board. As I looked through the various teaching positions around the world, I found that most required a number of certificates or degrees. But then I discovered the link that would change my life:

*Teaching Opportunity in Sudan. Must Fill Immediately!*

I clicked on it and read eagerly, "No experience required. Room, board, and travel paid in full. Teachers needed for immediate placement at British Educational Schools."

I'd never given Sudan a second thought. All I knew of it was in regards to the violence that had erupted in 2003 in Darfur, but I had no real connection to it. After some research, I found that Sudan, bordered by Egypt to the north, was a third world country and the largest in both the Arab and African worlds (nearly one-third the size of the U.S. and more than one million square miles), and Arabic was the prominent language. Overall, there were over one hundred different indigenous languages spoken in Sudan, including Nubian, Ta Bedawie, and dialects of Nilotic and Nilo-Hamitic languages.

Khartoum was the capital and located at the joining of the White Nile, which flows north from Lake Victoria, and the Blue Nile, flowing west from Ethiopia. From there, the Nile continues to flow north towards Egypt and the Mediterranean Sea. Khartoum was mostly dry, desert country but spotted with the occasional oasis. In the south, along the Ugandan border, the region consisted of grasslands and dense forests with heavy rainfall, and a variety of wildlife, including crocodiles, hippos, elephants, giraffes, lions, and various poisonous reptiles.

At the time, Sudan was in the middle of a civil war, the longest in African history, which originated in southern Sudan, but had spread to the Nuba Mountains and Blue Nile. The Sudanese were fighting over resources, yes, but mostly? They were fighting over religion.

*How interesting*, I thought and read on.

Apparently, the southern Sudanese were fighting for their right to practice Christianity in a country governed by Sharia, the strictest form of Islamic law, based on the code of law in the Qur'an. The war had been raging for twenty-one years, had killed two million people, and had displaced another four million.

Online articles portrayed Sudan as a place of indescribable horrors executed on a brutally hot desert with more pyramids than Egypt and unscathed archeological sites, including prehistoric tombs in the east that ranged sixteen yards in diameter and were dated to the fifth millennium BCE.

As nuts as it sounds, I was intrigued by it all: the danger, the fight for religious freedom, the pyramids, and even the morbid landscape. I reasoned that Indiana Jones had been in many dangerous places, like the Temple of Doom in India. Sure, he'd almost had his heart ripped out by a Kali-worshiping Thuggee cult, but good god, look how exciting that was! I didn't believe the Indiana Jones movies portrayed real-life depictions of people from faraway lands—not at all. But I did trust that a new culture would bring real-life adventure, and that's all I was looking for.

I emailed the headmistress of British Educational Schools: Fifi, a British woman who'd been living in Sudan for over five years. She seemed friendly enough and I trusted her (rather naively) when during a phone interview she said, "No need to worry! Khartoum's one of the safest cities in all of Africa. There's very little violence here."

But even if I'd known this wasn't the case, what she said next had me hooked and there was no going back.

"Please be aware that due to Sharia law, you can't legally buy or drink alcohol here. So if you're looking for a party or club-type atmosphere this isn't the place for you."

Did I hear her right?

"Alright, let's do it."

Sudan had all the requirements of an Artemis adventure along with the added bonus of no temptation of getting drunk. And that's all it took: a little imagination, a little trust, some internet research, and *boom*, I was on my way.

***

"What do you mean you're going to Sudan?" my parents asked when I broke the news.

I had planned on giving it to them gently, but instead I heaved the news all over the place leaving them flabbergasted and pale in the face. I was nervous about the conversation that would follow, and considering our history, I had a right to be.

"Didn't I read somewhere that Sudan was nominated as the third most dangerous country in the world?"

My dad was talking about a recent article published by *Forbes*, which I was aware of and yes, it had listed Sudan as the third most dangerous country in the world.

"Dad, Sudan is more than a million square miles. The civil war and genocide are *very* far away from Khartoum. There's no need to worry."

This information didn't appear to be helping the matter and I figured it wouldn't. We were a trio of somber soldiers addicted to the struggle, and I'd packed a can of knock-out gas so I could render them unconscious at the first sign of a struggle.

Okay, not really—but I did have my defenses up and was posed for a fight. Yet now that the moment was here, my heart softened. All I wanted was their support. This was all I'd ever wanted from them, but I had no idea how to ask for it anymore.

"Listen, I'm all signed up. I've sent the contract to the headmistress and my visa should be here in a few weeks."

An awkward silence.

"If you're sure this is what you want to do, we'll do everything we can to help you get there."

A white flag from Mom.

They stood up from the couch, shoulders hunched, looking small. It appeared they had no fight left in them—and thank God, because I was exhausted. We put down our armor and embraced, a silent agreement that for now we would surrender without a victor or a resolution.

"We love you, Shannon."

As a kid, I had deeply resented these words. It was hard to believe them because from my perspective their love appeared conditional. Maybe this *was* the case and my anger toward them was justified all those years. But now that I've matured some, I can see the gray area Dr. Reynolds talked about. In it, there is a lot to consider, such as my parent's side of the story and the fact that they both came from very abusive homes. My parents didn't have easy access to all the resources available now, like Oprah and her Super Soul Sunday shows or the internet to help locate a therapist qualified in trauma-informed care with Google reviews to back him or her up. Back then it was uncommon to even consider the effects of mental, physical, and emotional abuse on a child, let alone seek support for it.

In my younger years, I found it hard to grasp any of this until I started to become abusive too. Most people don't know this, but sometimes when I got overly intoxicated, I'd do more than just hit, slap, and bite. One time, in a rage, I dragged a friend around by her hair. Just like my mom did to me when I was four years old. Dr. Reynolds helped me make this connection. At first, I had a hard time accepting what I'd done. But he suggested that by practicing forgiveness for my mom's behavior, I'd eventually be able to forgive my own.

"Imagine your mom as a child and it will be easier for you. Most likely violence was a norm for her growing up. She adapted and wasn't allowed to ask questions. Later, as an adult parent, your mom abused you, her child—whom she loves and adores—because she believed that the punishments acted out on her were done out of love. This is what she was told. Your mom was probably unaware that the violence she endured was directly related to the fact that *her parents were beaten also*. And now here you are today, Shannon, carrying the pattern forward."

This was some pretty heavy stuff for a girl teetering between the scriptures and drink-all-day-every-day. But skipping ten years into the future, I can create a new visual: I am in Las Vegas with my family for Thanksgiving, where my parents are serving a Mormon mission. We're laughing, cooking, and playing games. I'm not a member of their church and yet I'm supportive of their dedication to it, and I appreciate its teachings—especially its focus on family togetherness—and my parents are supportive and appreciative of me outside the church. There is no armor, no war. We're working hard to understand our struggles and to nurture a relationship based on understanding and compassion. I've been able to forgive them for the past and instead of throwing blame in their direction, I've worked hard to recognize my own part in it. Trust me, as an addicted person I contributed a great deal to the chaos and pain that took place in our family during those earlier years.

On the day I broke the news about my trip, our relationship was an open wound resembling a grossly infected and swollen sliver, a result of constant picking with the wrong set of tools and a result of neglect. On that day there was nothing I could do but say goodbye and there was nothing they could do but let me go. Yet regardless of the toxic state of our relationship, my parents kept their promise and did everything they could to ensure I arrived in Sudan with all the essentials. It was an act of unconditional love that I couldn't see at the time, but I do now and so I thank you, Mom and Dad.

I love you, too.

***

The trip to Sudan was long and taxing, a whirlwind of New York, Germany, and Qatar, three intensely different environments, and I got whiplash trying to take it all in. Finally, though, I was flying high to Sudan.

As I boarded that last flight, it dawned on me that I was not Artemis, but Shannon, this really inexperienced girl from Utah, who didn't have a clue about war zones or Islam or world travel. I'd never even been outside the U.S. before. And there I was sitting on a plane that would, in less than an hour, descend into Africa.

"What are you thinking dude? Are you insane?"

It was Doubting Shan, a nasty voice in my head that I knew all too well. She'd been with me since my teenage years when

I had been told that my dreams were silly and it was best not to pursue them. Her cruel take on the world and my worth usually led me to drink.

"Yeah, you haven't got a clue! How are you going to deal with 'the wild' when you've never really been on your own? Plus, you're a lush!" Punk Shan said, and she was just as bad as Doubting Shan—maybe worse.

They were all there, my Melancholy Posse: Doubting Shan, Punk Shan, Scaredy-Cat Shan and Give Me a Vodka Shan. I was powerless to this crew and there was nothing I could do but let them drag me down into their gloomy lair of misery and wretchedness.

"Can't you guys just leave me alone? The plane will land in an hour. I can't deal with this right now!"

"What if you get raped? Murdered?" Scaredy-Cat Shan said. "What if you're taken hostage? What if you contract malaria and die? Or what if you get bilharzia from the water like the travel doctor said? Do you want worm eggs hatching in your brain, Shan?"

I hadn't slept in days and my nerves were a bundle of frazzled wires and loose connections. Any minute a circuit breaker was sure to blow. The last thing I needed was Scaredy-Cat Shan freaking me out with thoughts of worm babies squirming around in my head. Of course I already knew that these were my fears, which I'd been suppressing for obvious reasons.

"You can't suppress your feelings forever, Shannon. Don't you ever learn?" Punk Shan said.

It was no use, so I let everything surface all at once. I'd smoked way too much pot back in the day and would never be able to think clearly. My coping skills were a wreck. This was, hands down, the most dangerous and ridiculous thing I'd ever done. I was going to die out there, all alone, a clueless, stupid girl.

"Maybe we should have one last drink before we land. It'll help us relax," Give Me a Vodka Shan said.

"Really? And have her show up drunk to a war-torn country? Don't be ridiculous!" Punk Shan said.

"Enough!" I shouted.

That shut them up. I tried to take a deep breath to calm myself down, but nothing came of it. My throat constricted.

Not now, I thought.

But it was too late. A panic attack was about to hit like a tornado hits a house: fast and unexpected.

I bent over and tried blocking out the noise of the plane and the person sitting beside me. A handful of worst-case scenarios whirled around my head like the Wicked Witch of the West, cackling and insulting. Oddly, the most terrifying thoughts had nothing to do with dying in Sudan, but dying before I got there. I feared the plane would suddenly drop from the sky or I'd lose my passport and they wouldn't let me enter, or the job would no longer be available and I'd be sent packing. I didn't know why this journey felt so necessary, but I was desperate for it.

I got up quickly and made my way to the bathroom, where I sunk to the floor in a messy, teary heap. I heaved for air, my chest screaming in agony when none could be found. It seemed now was as good a time as any to pray to my God, the one from my early years, who I'd never forgotten but hadn't reached out to in a really long time.

After a long, quiet moment, when I was finally able to catch my breath, I looked up like I did as a kid and said:

"Hello. You. I know it's been a while, but it'd be really cool if you could come on this adventure with me, so I'm not completely alone. I'll need a friend, you know? Someone to help me find my way..."

I sat there for a while, waiting for the tornado to subside. When it did, as all storms do, I pulled myself up, dusted myself off, and waited for Khartoum.

# Chapter 3

When I stepped off the plane and onto Sudan's sherbet-orange desert, the sun sucker-punched me in the gut and then did a drop-jab to the jugular as if it were Floyd Mayweather and we'd suddenly entered into a boxing match. Stunned and defenseless, I doubled over.

I moaned, struggling to breathe.

If this is what 120 degrees felt like—Sudan's typical weather forecast—this test of survival was going to be a lot harder than I'd planned on. Just breathing while carrying my bags and walking to the airport was agony. I tried catching my breath so I wouldn't pass out; it was tricky.

But I made it. Once inside, I was twenty-two again and sitting front and center at a Creed concert with Scott Stapp's heavenly sweat spraying all over me. My eyes were wide with disbelief over the fact that *this was really happening*, and it was all I could do to keep from pumping my fists in the air to celebrate the vastness of the moment. For most, the Khartoum International Airport was probably pretty lame. There were ten workers sitting at a cut-rate table under a barely working fan. The men were in white *jellabiyas*, a traditional Muslim garment native to the Nile Valley, and they had turbans on their heads. The women were wearing bright, sparkly wraps known as the Sudanese *tobe,* and each one had a *hijab* or Muslim veil draped around her head and chest.

Finally, Africa!

I didn't know a single person who'd ever set foot here. Friends and family weren't tagging themselves in a Khartoum Vacation Photo Album online. Considering the Department of State had urged U.S. citizens not to travel to Sudan, and on their website they'd listed the risks involved (random attacks on foreigners in the form of suicide operations, bombings, and kidnappings) it was safe to say that Sudan was not a vacation spot for many. The diehard adrenaline junky couldn't get in even if she wanted to—at least not without a work visa or special connections to someone on the inside.

I'd left everyone I'd known in the whole wide world behind, and the solitude felt like a gift. I couldn't wait for the chance to hear my innermost thoughts without the expectations and ideas of others crowding them out. I wondered what the journey would entail. What would I discover about myself? What were my strengths? My weaknesses? Would I be able to, as Dr. Reynolds had suggested, rewire my brain so it could one day be a tool for peace and love in my life?

Would I find the skills I needed to stay sober? Would I figure out where I fit in and how we were all connected?

I hoped so. These were things I thought about constantly. Over the years, I'd filled dozens of journals with similar questions, and I'd always felt it was important to try and figure it all out. In Sudan, I could be that kid again full of wonder with my pad and pencil in hand, investigating and taking notes. And I wouldn't let anybody steer me from my mission: to remain open, to try and grasp what was truly possible for one individual in a limitless world.

In that moment, I declared, as Alice did in Lewis Carol's *Wonderland*:

*This is MY dream. I'll decide where it will go from here.*

Even three weeks later, when everything was unraveling around me, my resolve was still intact.

***

*It's Sunday, September 5*[th]*, 2004,* I wrote enthusiastically in my crisp, new journal. I'd been writing almost every day since I got here, and as usual, I was sprawled on my stomach on the bedroom floor of my new home in Dem, a radically poor town in Khartoum. I'd opted for the floor because my bed was made of rough, scratchy tweed and was painful to the touch.

*I can't believe it! I've been here almost three weeks. School is starting soon but there are no supplies. How am I going to teach without books, paper, and pencils? Hello! Oh well, as the Sudanese say, "shwaya, shwaya."*

So far the phrase *shwaya, shwaya* (slowly, slowly) summed up my experience of Sudan perfectly. Well, that and the phrase *Insha'Allah* (if God wills). Both were used countless times per day in place of "perhaps one day" or "hopefully one day" when the truth of the matter was that it probably wasn't going to happen at all — so don't count on it. I found this fun.

"Shannon? You in there?" asked Adelaide, my roommate, a gorgeous girl who was both supermodel tall and supermodel slender. She'd come from the Bronx, was my age, and would also teach at British Educational Schools (BES). She wanted me to call her Addy for short, and Addy had the wildest, kinkiest auburn-colored curls I'd ever seen.

"Come on in."

Addy opened the door and poked her head through. "This is going to sound really weird, but is your hair falling out?"

I raised my eyebrows and twisted my neck to see her. Addy typically lived life on the edge of an imaginary cliff that she was connected to by make-believe rope. Some days the rope broke, and when it did, she'd plummet to the ground in a melodramatic crash. But most of the time she just hung there with her arms flailing around and her eyes protruding from her head. Her jade-colored eyes were really beautiful, except when she was in panic mode and they popped out a little too far, causing her to look like a character from *Beetlejuice*.

"Not that I'm aware of." I stroked my hair to double check. I had to handle Addy's freak-outs with extreme caution. If I didn't, we'd both end up in a strait jacket from stress.

She held up a massive clump of hair she'd obviously pulled out of our shower drain. It was the size of an orange.

"Whoa!"

"Yeah, I know. My hair's been shedding for like two weeks. I was hoping it would stop or that I was just imagining it." She paused and then added, "At this rate we'll both be bald soon."

"We?"

"A lot of this hair belongs to you."

I jumped to my feet to examine the evidence. *What?* Visions of Bald Shan danced through my head and I winced; she wasn't pretty.

"Why is this happening?" I asked.

"It could be a number of things—the water, the heat, the food. All of the above?"

I considered the options. If the culprit was indeed "all of the above," then we were royally screwed because all of the above was out of our control. The heat hadn't let up even a few degrees and the food and water came with an array of complicated issues we had no business trying to tackle.

"Maybe our hair is just shedding naturally in order to keep us cool. Like some weird biological response to the heat?" I suggested. Addy and I looked down at the hefty clump resting in her palm.

Or maybe it was the food and water. Our main problem was that we'd had to eat local because we couldn't afford anything prepackaged. Our salary was several thousand dinars per month and equaled about $120 at the time, which ended up being a very small amount (even for Khartoum) despite Fifi promising it would allow us to "live like queens in Sudan."

We could barely afford to buy the wilted produce at any of the nearby *suks* (markets), and ever since we'd eaten the Sudanese cuisine, which consisted of small cups of *shai* (tea) with heaping spoonfuls of sugar, *asida* (millet porridge), *kisra* (flat bread), *ful* (fava beans smothered in oil and goat cheese), and *tamia* (fried chickpeas), Addy and I had been losing an excessive amount of liquid. Uncomfortably.

My travel doctor, Dr. Gibbs, had warned me about this very thing: "Promise me you won't ever drink or eat the local food and water. The water is heavily polluted. Some say it's only *slightly* filtered from the Nile, which is filled with bilharzia and dead bodies. All the local produce will be fertilized and therefore contaminated by it."

Dr. Gibbs was impressed that I was going to Sudan—although she was skeptical about my going alone. In all her years in the profession, she'd never known anybody to travel there, so she made me promise one more thing.

"Send me a postcard from Khartoum?"

I had promised her I'd do both without realizing that trying to find a postcard in non-touristy Sudan would be like trying to find toilet paper in a country without proper plumbing systems. Which was my next predicament: our shower situation. The water we used to shower with came from a water pump on our roof. From the roof, the water was heated by Sudan's heat-hyper sun and funneled down into our shower system. The water was both scalding hot by the time it reached us and the color of diluted Tang, and it left a slimy residue on our seared skin.

"What are we going to do?" Addy asked, bringing me back to the present.

"We're going to have to do some research. Let's talk to the other teachers at the school and see if they've experienced anything like this." Most of the teachers at BES were well-traveled foreigners. I hoped they would know what was going on.

"I bet it's our shower water. Every time I get out, my head and skin itch. Maybe the water is just so polluted that it..." Addy stopped and let the sentence hang.

I shivered, unsure if I wanted her to finish.

***

*5:00 a.m.* That's when the *adhan,* the Islamic call to prayer, blasts from a nearby mosque. The *adhan* is recited by the resident *muezzin,* a man chosen for his ability to recite the call to prayer in perfect melodic harmony. It echoes throughout Khartoum five times a day, and when it does, all Muslims are required to stop what they are doing, face the direction of the Kaaba (a sacred building in Mecca), and bow on their knees to Allah. In time I would become so accustomed to the *adhan* carrying on during the day that I'd become unfazed by it. But during those first few months? Not so much.

"*Allahu akbar,*" wailed the *muezzin.* "*As-salatu Khavrun Minan-nawm.*" *God is greatest. Prayer is better than sleep.*

I jerked from my slumber, my heart thrashing about. This is how I woke up every morning and then I'd lie back down on my tweed bed and give myself a pep talk.

*Go back to sleep, Shan. It's just the call to prayer...*

But it was impossible to fall back to sleep because Addy couldn't fall back to sleep. She'd jump out of bed the moment the *adhan* blasted and start clanking pots and pans in the kitchen as if she were Steven Adler from Guns N' Roses (although she looked more like Slash with her head of poufy curls) instead of boiling water for coffee. All we could afford was a small and imported (and therefore expensive) box of Nescafé, so every morning we'd drink it slowly in order to savor every drop. It was, after all, the only normal thing we'd taste on our lips all day and the only thing that didn't make us sick.

On that particular morning I was in a mood even though I should've been ecstatic. It was the first day of school and I would finally get to meet my students. The problem was that I had overheard some pretty concerning things while hanging around BES in order to get to know the teachers and learn the ropes of the country—one being that the kids were stuck-up elitists and belonged to wealthy and well-traveled ambassadors and diplomats, and the other being that the teachers were expected to give good grades to everyone regardless of their performance.

I was also apprehensive because the school supplies still hadn't arrived and Fifi was adamant that I produce two months' worth of lesson plans for her by the end of the week. I got the feeling she didn't like me and I wasn't sure why. She was cold and distant like an iceberg, and so were the other teachers at the school. They'd given the cold shoulder to Addy too, and I thought maybe it was because we were young and American. Most of the teachers at the school were older and from Europe or they were Sudanese Arab Muslims or Sudanese African Christians. Whatever it was, it was clear that Addy and I were the outsiders.

"Morning, Miss Addy," I said, rubbing the slumber from my eyes as I greeted her in the kitchen doorway. Teachers at BES were addressed by their first names.

"Hello, Miss Shannon. Your coffee is on the table. I'm going to hop in the shower."

Drowsy, I slumped into a plastic chair at our plastic dining table and yawned while appreciating a deep overhead stretch. Our new home stood three stories tall, was made of concrete, and compared to the tiny shacks scattered around it, it looked outrageous and out-of-place. It was a gaudy monstrosity in this poor town— though in America it'd be considered a dump. Inside, it was empty except for a dining table, our beds, and wardrobes. The first floor was decked out in all white: white tile, white walls, white ceiling. When cleaned, it sparkled, but it was hardly ever clean because Sudan's rough-grained desert would sneak its way in through various nooks and crannies, accompanied by an interesting array of lizards, giant-fanged ants, and the occasional scorpion. When a *haboob* hit—a thick sandstorm carried on an atmospheric gravity current that blew in the deserts of North Africa and Arabia—it was hard to tell the outside from the inside.

The second floor of our home was a mess of concrete and wire, and the third was a roof, which we sat on to enjoy Sudan's skyline of towering, colorful mosques and a unique bird's-eye view of the homes next to ours. Most had broken roofs or half-roofs or no roofs at all, and so we could see Sudanese families cooking, braiding hair, applying henna to their hands, and taking naps on dirt floors.

After we were done with coffee and showers, Addy and I headed to BES, a small, one-story building painted an odd blue with low ceilings, narrow hallways, and cramped classrooms. BES was located near the corner of *Shar'ea Wahit wa* Mohammed Nageeb, and across from Ozone, a popular eatery that served pizza and French fries. Since Sudan was once colonized by Great Britain, the city streets are laid out in the shape of a Union Jack— not ideal for heavy traffic. The history between the Sudanese and the British is quite hostile. At one point, Kitchener, a field marshal who won his fame in 1898 for winning the Battle of Omdurman and securing control of Sudan, wanted to dig up the body of Muhammad Ahmad bin Abd Allah, a religious leader who claimed, in 1881, that he was the "Mahdi," the messianic redeemer of the Islamic faith—all so that Kitchener could turn the Mahdi's skull into an ashtray.

Since we couldn't afford a rickshaw or an *umjot* (taxi van), Addy and I had to travel to BES on foot, and although the walk was short—twenty minutes—it felt long and taxing. First we had to get past our neighbors who were asleep in their beds outside of our front door. (I understood why. Who could sleep indoors without air-conditioning?)

*"Ahlan, salam aleikum. Sabah al khair?"* two tired men greeted us with toothless grins. Most of our neighbors didn't speak English, but there were many on the streets of Khartoum who did.

*"Aleikum salam! Sabah al noor. Kaef?"* Peace and good morning to you. You okay?

In Addy's back pocket was an Arabic manual we practiced with every day. However, this was proving pointless since the manual highlighted Egyptian Arabic, and Sudanese Arabic is more closely related to Western Arabian Arabic, a dialect spoken in the Hejaz region in Saudi Arabia. Although both dialects share similar characteristic properties, Sudanese Arabic is considered a pure, archaic form, and the Sudanese spoke using older sounds not covered in our manual, so we had to learn everything by ear.

Some of the sounds were tricky, such as the antiquated *qaf* sound, which requires voiceless uvular plosive. To create this sound one had to obstruct airflow from their vocal track and then use the throat and tongue in a combination that felt very peculiar. At first try, Addy and I sounded (and probably looked) like Tweedle Dee and Tweedle Dum—perhaps British pirate versions that had a chunk of chewing tobacco lodged in the back of their throats. When we spoke, nobody had a clue what was going on, including us. I found this fun, too.

*"Kaef, tamam! Miya miya?"* I'm good. You good?

*"Alhamdullilah, tamam a tamam. Kaef?"* Thank Allah. I'm very good. Are you good?

*"Tamam! Inti kwayesa?"* Good! How are you?

*"Shukran jizelan. Miya miya. Inta kwayes?"* Thank you very much. I'm excellent! Are you good?

Sudanese greetings could last for days; it was time to cut this one short. We didn't have time. We had to get to class! So we bid them adieu and shuffled along. The rest of the walk was draining because the Sudanese couldn't stop staring at us. To them we were a couple of alien rock stars that had just stepped off a spaceship from the Great Beyond. Due to the strict visa restrictions, there were very few foreigners in Sudan, and none but us were living in their poor neighborhood. The only time they ever saw a foreigner was in the company of an expat entourage sitting pretty in a big SUV with the letters UNDP on the side, which stood for the United Nations Development Program, the lead development agency in Sudan working to facilitate a peaceful transition from recovery to development in line with national priorities.

The fact that I was wearing a hot pink t-shirt with the word *Diva* sprawled across my enormous breasts certainly wasn't helping the matter. It was a fashion *faux pas* that became obvious only after I'd landed in this North African Islamic city. My diva shirt was the epitome of all the shirts I'd brought because they were the only lightweight t-shirts I could find on short notice. This was one of the few tips Fifi offered; she also advised that I bring long skirts to combat the heat. So that's what I did. However, anytime I leaned over or raised my arms my shirt would lift up, and expose a half-inch of belly and/or back. In America, this isn't a big deal, so I'd thought nothing of it until a woman ran up to me on my first day in Khartoum and yanked my shirt down, hard.

*"Haram!" Forbidden!* she snapped.

My skirts hung two inches above my ankles, and ankles were also *haram*. It was an honest oversight, but I was being punished for it every day. The women especially treated me badly. I felt like Courtney Love *and* Britney Spears during the head-shaving incident, rolled into one big ball of train-wreck awesomeness. As I walked down their streets, the Sudanese women scowled at me.

On a positive note, the street kids thought I was pretty cool. Every morning they'd run up and twirl around me in circles.

"What's my name? What's my name?" they'd call out in broken English with stunning, bright smiles. They were totally adorable.

I liked the main road in Dem too. It was called *Shar'ea* Mohammed Nageeb and it was a vibrant tapestry interlaced with bursts of color and bustling activity: street dogs and children ran amok, white-turbaned merchants peddled knickknacks, jet-black southerners loomed tall as the lime green minarets, beetle-shaped rickshaws zoomed, neon *tobed* women sipped tea at the curbside, colorful plastic trash bags hung from tree branches like rainbow-colored cherry blossoms, and legless beggars scuttled through clouds of orange dust, which swirled *everywhere*.

The dust was so bad that I'd had to stop wearing contacts altogether because it would get trapped beneath them. At times it felt as if the sand were actually trying to scrape off the top layer of both eyeballs, which was not cool. Since I didn't bring any glasses with me, it was hard to see, especially in a *haboob*, and this was risky since most of Dem's streets were littered with seven-foot potholes.

Overall, I found Khartoum—spectacularly set at the joining of the Blue Nile and the White Nile—and its hodge-podge of city folk *delightful*. But I sensed pain too. It hung on the breath of every living thing. I'd been learning a little more about the civil war, which had erupted in 1983 and was known as the Second Sudanese Civil War. So far it had one of the highest civilian death tolls of any war since World War II and was marked by a disturbingly large number of human rights violations, including slavery, ethnic cleansing, and mass killings. This was at the hands of their own government, which had imposed a harsh brand of Sharia on all the Sudanese regardless of their religious stance. Punishments included public flogging, lashing, amputations, and hangings for crimes like public affection, premarital sex, theft, and political opposition.

In Sudan, religious differences had created a great divide. The darker-skinned Christian African southerners were the underdogs, and the tension between they and the lighter-skinned Muslim Arab northerners was paramount in almost every interaction. Yet it was a very interesting time to be here: the genocide had only recently erupted in Darfur and it was garnering a great deal of media exposure for the entire country. Plus, there was talk of a possible peace agreement to integrate all religions into Sudanese society and end the civil war—although I'd been told not to get too invested in this since peace talks had been going on for over a decade. Still, I was interested to see what would come of it.

By the time we reached BES, I was overwhelmed by the smell of rotting trash in the open sewer systems that ran along *Shar'ea* Mohammed Nageeb, sights of femur bones at Farouk Cemetery, which had been uncovered by the *haboob*, and my newfound fame with the Sudanese. I headed straight to the toilet to vomit.

\*\*\*

Full of life, my students burst into the classroom with giant grins splashed across their faces. There were nine of them: Saara, Rashida, Sharifa, Dalila, Fatima, Yusif, Ebrahim, Mohammed, and Joseph, and they were nothing like the little punks they'd been made out to be. As third-graders, they were at the fun and innocent ages of six, seven, and eight. They threw their school bags on the floor with great enthusiasm, ran up to my waist with outstretched arms, and then bombarded me with a million questions all at once, just like I used to do to my dad:

"Are you our teacher?"

"My mum said you're from America! Are you?"

"Do you know P. Diddy and Alicia Keys?"

"Do they have snow where you're from?"

"What it's like in America?"

Their energy was infectious; more effective even than a shot of Ethiopian coffee, and that stuff was strong. I forgot my stomach problems instantly. I loved kids. Back home, I usually sat at the kids' table with my nieces and nephews during family dinners. I found their excitement and curiosity for life refreshing.

"Hello, everyone! I'm Miss Shannon. Yes, I'm from America, but no, I don't know P. Diddy or Alicia Keys, although that would be really, really cool. I'm from Utah, which is next to California, and we get tons of snow in the winter. In fact, I grew up snowboarding. Does anybody know what that is?"

The kids shook their heads without taking their eyes off me. This was how it would be throughout the school year. They'd treat me like the kids on *Shar'ea* Mohammed Nageeb did, and I would be their rock star.

"Find a seat and I'll draw a picture on the board to show you."

The kids sat down and I picked up a piece of chalk and began to draw a mountain with a snowboarder at the top and a bubble with the words "Watch out below!" inside. Then I drew an innocent bystander standing at the bottom of the hill right in the snowboarder's path.

"Okay, so this is a snowboard and this is the snow. You stand on top of this and go down the hill like this. Now, see this person here? He is about to be smashed flat by this snowboarder girl if he doesn't get out of the way—and quick!" I drew an X over the guy and dramatic swirls to indicate he'd been smooshed.

"Teacher!" Fatima said, looking bewildered.

"What? It's a joke!" I said. That's another thing about kids. They brought out my goofy side.

The kids didn't get my sense of humor—yet. But over time they would, and we'd spend our days giggling, learning, teasing, and at times getting into serious trouble with the other teachers for being too loud. The materials would show up, *insha'Allah,* so we had to make up our lesson plans together. I let them choose the countries they wanted to learn about for geography and which books they wanted to read in class. We even ended up learning a bit of French together just because we could. I found everything I needed to know online in the teacher lounge or at a local internet café.

Our class was entertaining and spontaneous—a safe haven from the outside world, which was rapidly falling apart.

\*\*\*

Friday was a holy day for Muslims, and most spent it at the mosques gathered in reverent prayer. For Addy and I, Fridays represented the end of a long workweek and we celebrated by roasting coals over our portable kitchen stove and carrying them up to the roof along with our hookah and two plastic chairs for an evening of tobacco and conversation.

Under the dusk sky we puffed away while discussing the week's events. Last week's discussion had revolved around the random power outages that made it hard to boil water and left us starving. On this day, Addy's main concern was our hair. It was still shedding at an alarming rate and we'd both done our research. One teacher said it happened to her and then suddenly stopped, and another said her eyebrows fell out when she first got here and never grew back. Neither of us had a clue what was going on and lately it was all Addy could talk about, and her obsession was quickly becoming my own. I found it impossible to wake up without immediately counting out the strands of loose hair in my hand. A few days ago, I'd gone to the local internet café and googled the typical rate of hair loss and discovered that I was shedding more than the average.

After we had nothing left to say on this topic, we sat in silence. Puffing pensively, I debated whether or not to share a juicy bit of new information with Addy since getting her all riled up was exhausting for us both. But I figured, why not? This is what our time together was all about these days: scaring the shit out of each other.

"Svetlana thinks we've been cursed by black magic. She says that's what happened to her when she first got to Sudan and that's why she has those boils all over her face."

Svetlana, a woman from Transylvania, a region in the central part of Romania, had converted to Islam, married a Sudanese man, and now taught at BES. I told Addy that according to Svetlana, Sudanese women used black magic to cast the evil eye on other women out of jealousy and envy. Svetlana had also mentioned a common and fascinating Sudanese custom known as the *Zar*, which took place whenever someone—typically a woman—was possessed by evil spirits and included hiring an exorcist.

Belief in magic is widespread throughout Africa and especially in the Sub-Sahara and surrounding areas. Witch doctors are consulted for a variety of reasons, such as healing diseases, political and financial gain, help with a person's love life, and placing hexes on people who pissed you off. In Sudan, one can easily find a witch doctor, spiritualist, or black magic healer to assist with the removal of evils spells. According to Svetlana the hex removal process, which could only be done by a healer, typically took seven days.

"I guess you can buy all sorts of black magic charms at any of the *suks,* and they're typically made out of dead animal parts."

Addy puffed on this news and then added in her own gossip. "You know that guy Daniel that works over at the shop? He thinks we're being watched."

"By who?"

"The government. He says he's seen people following us around. And then when I went to the internet café the other day, I found that both our names had been typed into Google, like somebody had been researching *us.*"

I puffed uneasily. It was my turn.

"You know the tall British teacher at BES? The one that always has a briefcase in one hand and looks like a southerner? He's been arrested like five times in the last year. The police keep mistaking him for a Sudanese witch doctor."

"A witch doctor?"

"Apparently there is a Sudanese witch doctor going around Khartoum and...stealing penises."

"What?!"

"I know, it's crazy, but that's what he said. He puts the stolen penises in his briefcase."

"And how does he get the penises?"

"With a handshake."

"A handshake."

"Yup."

"Seriously? What's with these people and shaking hands?"

"I think it's safe to say, just don't shake anybody's hand around here. *Ever.*"

We snickered. Shaking with your left hand is a serious taboo because it is what one uses to wipe with whenever the water shuts off and renders the bidet useless. I didn't know this on my first day in Khartoum and had offered my left hand to my new neighbor because I was holding a suitcase with my right. After the look I got, I knew I'd never forget this very significant cultural norm.

That night the moon sat large and luminous in the sky with its bottom lit up so that it perfectly resembled the grin of Cheshire Cat. I'd never seen the moon like this before since it happened rarely and depended on latitude. It was pure magic because after all, I was Alice, magnificently content in my Wonderland as I blew out Os into the sky like Aslan, her wise and prickly caterpillar friend.

"Have you seen them?" Addy asked after an extended silence. "The police guys with Kalashnikov rifles? I saw them setting up roadblocks near the bus station the other day."

"I know. Something's going on."

"I've asked around but nobody is talking. Whatever it is, they don't want us to know."

The U.S. Passports and International Travel website had also warned of "violent flare-ups" and "demonstrations in Khartoum" that could happen with "little notice."

"How curious," I said and blew out another O, feeling perfectly freaked out and perfectly alive.

# Chapter 4

"**S**HANNON!"

I bolted upright from a hot, dizzy sleep drenched in sweat. I'd been dreaming the *muezzin* was calling my name from atop a minaret, my fame having reached new heights that not even Oprah could touch.

I rolled onto my side and groaned. My back was killing me. Sleeping on my tweed bed was like sleeping on literal pins and needles.

"SHANNON!"

It wasn't a dream. It was Addy once again at my bedroom door. Her voice said *trouble* and I jumped out of bed on high alert.

"What's wrong?" I asked as I let her in. She practically fell on top of me with her *Beetlejuice* eyes bulging. She'd just come back from an early morning jog, which we usually ran together, but I hadn't felt well that morning and slept in.

"We've got to get out of here."

"Why? What happened?"

She paced around the room, jittery and manic. It looked as if she were being electrocuted. Her tight curls were sticking straight out.

"Tell me!" I said and grabbed her arm. As she faced me, I saw that her eyes were filled with fear.

"I was jogging along Africa Road, minding my own business like we do every morning, right? And this police officer, *shorta*— whatever!—comes out of nowhere and orders me to stop. *Then he put a gun to my head and forced me on my knees."*

I stared at her.

"I thought he was going to rape or shoot me right there."

"How'd you get away?"

"I told him I was an American and I didn't know about the curfew."

I grimaced. First, the American card was a tricky play. The relationship between the U.S. and Sudan hadn't been in the best shape after Sudan declared war on Israel in the 60s and later backed Iraq in its invasion of Kuwait in the 90s while allegedly providing protection and assistance for Islamic terrorist groups. Following the first World Trade Center bombing in 1993, the U.S. State Department noted that five of fifteen suspects were Sudanese. The States' punishment for Sudan? Sanctions and a spot on the sponsor-of-terrorism list. The U.S. had even bombed Sudan's Al-Shifa pharmaceutical factory in 1998 (codenamed Operation Infinite Reach) alongside terrorist bases in Afghanistan in retaliation for bombing American embassies in Kenya and Tanzania. The missiles were launched from American warships in the Red Sea and the U.S. claimed that Osama bin Laden—the man supposedly behind the embassy bombings—was using the factory to build chemical weapons.

Second, *curfew?*

We ran on Africa Road nearly every morning at this hour and we'd never had any problems. Damn those teachers at BES for not keeping us informed!

Addy, clearly shaken up, began to ramble on and on about danger and dying, but I had to tune her out. I couldn't focus. What did this mean? Should we leave the country? *Can* we leave? How do we get out? Who will help us get out? Certainly not our informative "friends" at the school. My head pounded with intense pressure. I had no idea how to deal with this or what to think. I'd never lived in a war zone before!

I boiled us two cups of Nescafé. We didn't want to venture out while the curfew was still in place so we sipped it slowly and waited for the sun to come up. Once it was, we hopped on a rickshaw in order to get to the school faster and arrived in under five minutes. Frazzled and out of sorts, we hunted for the only person in Khartoum that might be able to help us: Khaled. We figured that Khaled, an American who had converted to Islam and moved to Sudan from California just a few years ago, would have a little compassion for two young Americans. He'd tell us what was up.

We found Khaled in the teacher lounge relishing some plum-colored olives and a slab of goat cheese. This pissed off Addy and she lunged for him.

"Khaled, why don't you tell us what's going on around here? A police officer put a gun to my head this morning because of some curfew that we know nothing about."

Khaled sat up and put his fingers to his lips. "Girls! You can't talk about this stuff in the open."

Addy and I looked at each other wide-eyed. *What stuff?*

Khaled shoved his breakfast in his mouth and motioned for us to huddle up. Like American footballers, we crouched down and moved in close so we could hear him as he began to explain that earlier in the year Hassan al-Turabi, an enemy of the current President, Omar al-Bashir, was placed on house arrest because, allegedly, he tried to overthrow Bashir with the help of

Darfurian rebels. Turabi is considered one of the most influential figures in Sudanese politics, and he was hugely instrumental in institutionalizing Sharia. And Bashir? He has been voted (on numerous occasions and by various publications) one of the world's worst dictators. Case in point: Bashir is the only sitting head of state ever to face charges of genocide brought by the International Criminal Court.

"This is the juicy part," Khaled said. "Once upon a time, Bashir and Turabi were actually great allies. We're talking best buddies. Turabi was instrumental in helping Bashir gain power in a 1989 coup *and* he served as Bashir's right-hand man for an entire decade."

"What's this got to do with the curfew?" asked Addy.

"Turabi's off house arrest and the rumor is he's trying to overthrow Bashir. He wants revenge."

"Why'd Turabi try to overthrow Bashir in the first place?" I asked.

"Power? Jealousy? Who knows? But obviously Bashir isn't taking it lightly. He imprisoned Turabi twice already and had his followers completely purged from the government."

The feud between Bashir and Turabi is rumored to be mostly due to Turabi's links to Islamic fundamentalist groups while allowing them to operate out of Sudan, and then for personally inviting Osama bin Laden to move his base of operations to Sudan from Saudi Arabia in 1991. While bin Laden lived in Sudan, Turabi provided him a safe and friendly haven to conduct jihadist activities in exchange for his help in building roads and fighting against Christians and animists in southern Sudan.

Addy butted in. "My main concern is that nobody is keeping us in the loop. We don't have TV or radio, and even if we did, we don't understand the language. How can we protect ourselves if we don't have all the facts?"

"Like this curfew that's suddenly in place. Why didn't you guys tell us about it?" I asked.

"I understand your frustration," Khaled said. "But you have nothing to worry about. Just lay low and don't break curfew. *Ma mushkilla*."

*No problem.*

His comment was enough to push Addy off her imagined cliff and into free fall. Her arms went up. "That's our point! Tell me please, how we can 'lay low' and keep from breaking the curfew when nobody is informing us there is a curfew?"

"You want all the facts?" Khaled said and then turned to me. "Miss Shannon, there's something you should probably know. The little boy in your class, Yusif? He's a close relative of Turabi and his family is most likely involved in the coup. Yusif told me during lunch the other day that his dad brought him and his brother an Uzi and a Bazooka back from Europe recently. He assured me that the guns were very real. Whatever happens in your class, that boy needs to get all As and you should probably watch your back. Don't talk about the coup or say anything remotely suspicious."

"Remotely suspicious? What does that even *mean*?"

The bell rang and Khaled stood up. "Ladies, it's time for class. Just lay low, okay?"

***

A few days later the entire city was in chaos. Sudanese security forces set up roadblocks all over the streets and searched vehicles and homes around the clock. I saw them confiscate weapons and arrest people by the truckload, ripping innocent-looking people from buses while screaming in their faces and waving guns. I looked forward to class more and more with each passing day. It was the only time I felt normal, that I could enjoy the simple things in life. For instance, kids being kids. Khaled's warning wasn't far from my thoughts, but Yusif was such a sweetheart. He seemed like a perfectly innocent eight-year-old boy who wouldn't harm a fly. He was always checking in to see if I needed anything, and he tried really hard to do his best in class. I adored him.

This day was a Thursday and my students looked forward to Thursdays because we'd have Show and Tell directly after lunch. They could hardly wait to display their personal treasures in front of the class.

Fatima went first and held up a floral-patterned bookmark that her mom brought her from the United Kingdom. Mohammed went next and he showed a Disney coloring book that he was super excited about. Saara shared a poem that she'd written just for the class. We were all in it and it was pretty hilarious. Then it was Yusif's turn. He carried an unusually large backpack to the front of the room. I could tell by the way he grunted that it was too heavy for him, but I was too preoccupied with grading the kids' latest math test to pay much attention. My mind was a million miles away when I heard the kids gasp.

I looked up to find Yusif with a shiny black gun in his hand. "It's a real Uzi. My dad got it for me in Germany."

Khaled's voice blasted through my head like the *adhan* at five a.m.: *Yusif assured me that the guns were very real.*

"Teacher! Teacher! Do you want me to show you how it shoots?"

Time stopped. My vision blurred. I heard Yusif talking eagerly. I heard the kids yell. Yet I was stuck in my chair and couldn't move. My limbs felt like two-hundred-pound bags of sand and they tingled uncomfortably. Yes, Yusif *appeared* to be an innocent child. But it was suddenly painfully obvious that he'd also been brought up in a corrupt family, and in a complicated country currently in the middle of a coup that his family might be involved with. I didn't know his intentions with the gun or anyone else's. Could it be a preemptive strike by his family to get the attention of both the Sudanese and U.S. governments? What better way to create more chaos on the streets, making it easier for Turabi to gain control, than to shoot a sweet American teacher with chipmunk cheeks? It was a brilliant plan; it was just too bad I was in it.

"Yusif, don't!" I shouted.

Yusif turned and pointed the gun in my direction. His usual cheery grin faded. Into what? Was that confusion on his face? Betrayal? His arm raised a bit so that the Uzi was now pointing at my forehead instead of my heart. If the gun was loaded the bullets would go directly through my skull.

My heart groaned in protest: *No, no, no. This isn't happening to me. Why is this happening to me?*

I considered my options. I could jump past his gun and out of the door in the blink of an eye. I couldn't run as fast as a bullet but maybe there was a way to distract his aim. I scanned the room for ideas and noticed the kids on the floor hiding under their desks. Would it be wrong to take off and leave them? Of course it would, but this was *my life* on the line. I didn't want to know what it was like to have a hot bullet smash into my head and my brain splatter all over the walls of our classroom — not for anybody.

I started to hyperventilate, and as cliché as it sounds, my life did flash before my eyes. During the replay, the one thing that stood out the most was that I had wasted so much time worrying about what everyone else thought of me instead of what *I* thought of me. Why hadn't I invested more time in my own ideas and dreams? Because really…what was the point of living if my life looked exactly like everybody else's? If only I'd dared to live more courageously, especially considering how short and fragile everything is.

"Miss Shannon!" Sharifa screamed, bringing me back to the present. She was under her desk and watching me closely. Her large brown eyes seemed to plead for me to take charge; she seemed to believe that I had the power to keep her safe.

Dammit, Sharifa. I didn't want to die, but the kids needed and trusted me. I had to stay and protect them if I could.

I stood up abruptly. The chair caught on the carpet and fell backwards. We all jumped. My legs were still tingly and full of sand, but at least they worked.

"Please, Yusif. Give me the gun."

"No, no. It's okay, Miss Shannon." The gun wavered in his hand and he lowered it so that it was right at my waist.

My heart and the clock ticked in unison.

*Thump, tick, thump, tock, thump, tick...*

I took two quick steps out of the way of the barrel. Two more steps and I was at Yusif's side. I didn't breathe until the gun was in my hand, and when it was—finally—I let out a long, strangled sigh.

"Teacher?" Yusif asked. He was shaking and his lower lip trembled.

His sensitive display reminded me of the time when the kids and I accidently got paint everywhere during a spontaneous art project. Acrylics ended up all over our clothes, the walls of our classroom, and even our faces. Unfortunately, the water had been off that day and so we had to use rubbing alcohol to remove it from our skin. It wasn't easy to get it off their light blue uniforms.

Yusif had acted nervous and when he told me why, my heart broke. "If this paint doesn't come off my father will beat me." I'd spent a good twenty minutes that day scrubbing his shirt as hard as I could because I couldn't stand the thought of him being hurt because of something I'd done, accident or not.

I wrapped my arms around him and gave him a tender hug. "It's okay, Yusif, the gun just scared us a bit because of all the stuff going on outside. You're okay. I promise."

He hugged me back still shaking. "Teacher, I didn't mean to." He trailed off.

"I know. This is my fault, you know? I'm not used to being around all these guns." I gave a little laugh to lighten the mood; God knows we could've cut through the tension inside this room with an electrical chainsaw.

After the kids settled down, I shoved the gun back in the bag and rushed down the hall to Fifi's office. I saw that she was at her desk through a crack in the door and poked my head in.

"Got a minute?"

She shook hers. "Sorry, busy." She pointed at the paperwork on her desk.

I pushed through the door anyway and noticed for the first time that, like Yusif, I was shaking.

"No, we need to talk. Now."

"Miss Shannon, really, this is inappropriate."

I pulled the gun half way out of the backpack so she could see it. She stood up and motioned for me to shut the door. Together we examined it while I filled her in on our little classroom adventure.

"It's real, but look you can see here it's loaded with a fake magazine," she said. "I hope that next time you will check these things out before you come charging into my office like this? Really, can't you handle yourself with a little more professionalism?"

The bathroom I threw up in so often was just down the hall so I ran to it, shut the door, and slid to my butt with my head in my hands. It was a similar scene to the one in the bathroom on the flight over, and as if on cue my Melancholy Posse showed up and started in on me.

"Duh, Shan! It wasn't a real magazine. Talk about jumping to conclusions," Punk Shan said.

"I thought we were going to die!" Scaredy-Cat Shan shouted.

"This is why we drink, people! Who can cope with this crap?" Give Me a Vodka Shan said.

And then a gentler voice spoke up: "You guys, she's never held an automatic weapon before, and she didn't even know what a magazine was until now. Let's give her a break, huh?"

Silence.

The voice continued, "She could've run, but she stayed to protect those kids. Plus, she's *in* Sudan, *in* the middle of a coup, and it took a lot of courage to come here."

My Posse and I weren't used to someone going to bat for me. But this new voice, which I dubbed Peacemaker Shan, had a really good point. It had taken tremendous bravery to come here. Yes, it was risky, but at least I had dared to take a chance even though everyone told me I was ridiculous and stupid for it.

Then it struck me. In the eyes of the Mormons I'd always been considered a rebel without a cause. Was this true? Or was this label placed on me out of fear because they'd felt threatened by someone uninterested in living the very structured and very specific guidelines required of their members? I had a feeling that if *I* were to decide what was true about *me* as opposed to leaving this up to others to decide, then my self-perception, and therefore my self-esteem, would be healthier. Overall, I'd be a lot happier.

For the first time, I saw myself as a daring girl who was born to take risks, and considering the last few weeks, I was—in this moment—the most courageous person I knew.

\*\*\*

Addy and I prepared emergency kits and filled them with our passports, cash, bottled water, and snacks. We placed them under our beds in case we needed to run. The U.S. Embassy was too far away to get to on foot, so where would we go exactly? We didn't have that part figured out yet but at least we had essentials in case we needed to make a quick exit.

Bashir was all over the news. One day while at a local internet café, I overheard him say, "We truly applaud the citizens' cooperation and their patience regarding the security measures bothering everyone. But the harassment, which comes as a result of security measures, is easier for the people than the consequences which could arise as a result of a security breach."

I rolled my eyes at this. Patience and cooperation? Anyone with a Kalashnikov rifle pointed at her forehead would appear this way—don't you think, Bashir?

Addy and I were way past finding humor in our current situation. We'd taken Khaled's advice to the extreme and even quit our weekly rooftop hookah sessions. We couldn't risk the government spying on us or anyone trying to kidnap us, so we hid indoors. Out of sight, out of mind.

Yet life was still in session.

"We need to hit the *suk* or we'll starve. Let's take a rickshaw so we can get there faster?" I said.

Addy nodded. We'd been holed up in our rooms working on school stuff and I was starting to go stir crazy. A trip to the *suk* would be good for us. On the way to *Shar'ea* Mohammed Nageeb, we hurdled over potholes and a shiny stream of blood and guts that were oozing out of a gash in a dead goat's neck. Someone had skinned it, broken its legs, and tied it to a tree by its ruined limbs. This is how the Sudanese prepared fresh meat for special occasions, such as weddings and the *Eid al-Adha* (Feast of the Great Sacrifice) or the meal to break the Ramadan fast. Ramadan is an annual, worldwide fast and one of the Five Pillars of Islam, which are five basic and mandatory acts required of all Muslims. The other four Pillars include declaring there is no god except Allah and that Prophet Muhammad is God's Messenger, praying five times a day, giving a portion of one's savings to the poor, and pilgrimage to Mecca at least once in a lifetime. I'd seen enough animals slaughtered on these streets that the blood-spattered, pretzel-twisted goat didn't daunt me in the slightest.

At the *suk* we operated with the stealth and sophistication of two CIA agents. I grabbed the eggplant, cabbage, onions, and tomatoes. Addy grabbed the noodles, bread, goat cheese, and peppers. Done in under five minutes. We paid for our food, jumped back in another rickshaw, and gave the driver our address. He nodded and off we went—but in a direction opposite our home.

"This isn't our street! This isn't even the way!" Addy said, pointing at the dark alleyway we were headed toward.

"Where is he taking us?"

The driver picked up his pace and booked it toward a steep incline where a group of rickshaws were waiting at the top. The drivers were standing outside of their vehicles and facing us.

"Jump!" Addy screamed. Then she did just that. She jumped from the moving rickshaw.

Dumbfounded, I watched her fly out of the door, stumble down the hill, and take off running with her arms in the air.

*"Sa'adini!"* she yelled out as she ran. *Help me!*

I stalled, not quite sure what to do. I squinted to see the huddle ahead but everything was a blur without my contacts.

*She must have seen something serious?*

I jumped.

Then I twisted my ankle on a mound of dirt. It hurt.

"Addy!" I yelled and ran after her. She was already halfway down the hill by the time I caught up.

"Why are we running?"

Addy ignored me or didn't hear me. The expression on her face told me that she was in stealth mode and it was best not to disrupt her process. So I ran alongside her and watched as she bulldozed her way down the clumpy dirt hill and dashed over to a dark figure standing at the bottom. The sun had set so everything was shrouded in shadows.

"*Low samahtee*, can you help us? *Mumkin?*" Addy yelled at the figure, which turned out to be a woman wrapped in a light pink *obiya* (a Sudanese dress for unmarried women). Then she grabbed the woman's arm and spun her around.

Startled, the woman yanked her arm away and began screeching in Arabic. She shoved Addy so hard she almost fell backward.

"*La, la, la, la, la!*" I shouted. *No, no, no, no, no!* It was the only Arabic I could muster.

Addy apologized and in broken Arabic, she began to plead our case. "*Sakneen Shar'ea* Mohammed Nageeb *lacken* our rickshaw driver...*hua maznoon kateera! Yani, mafeesh hua leef yamen hena...*"

By piecing key words together, she was trying to explain that our "crazy" driver had turned here suddenly and we didn't know why, but in the process she'd called him crazy expensive. Frustrated by the language barrier, Addy turned and pointed at our rickshaw still stopped at the top of the hill.

"*Shufti!*" *Look!* she cried.

The confused woman looked to where Addy had pointed. Then she calmed some and waved her hands.

"*Kulu tamam,*" she said. *Everything is okay.*

The woman explained that *Shar'ea* Mohammed Nageeb was closed for the night because of the coup and the drivers were simply waiting for a traffic jam to clear up. I found it easier to understand Arabic when it was spoken to me than to actually speak it myself.

Embarrassed, we trudged back up the hill to the rickshaw we'd just jumped out of.

Our driver didn't seem pleased with us, but he let us back in. Under his breath he cursed us and I was okay with it because

he was right: we were absolutely a pair of foolish Americans.
I could own it without question, but I didn't want to tell him
because I was too drained from all the commotion. What had
just happened?

"Addy, why'd you jump?"

"I thought Osama bin Laden was trying to kidnap us."

"You thought *bin Laden* was trying to kidnap us?"

"Didn't you see what was written on the back of that rickshaw
at the top of the hill?"

We were close enough now that I could see a picture of Osama
bin Laden with his name in bold print beneath it. Bin Laden was
a hero to the Sudanese—not because he was an alleged terrorist
leader, but because he had invested over fifty million dollars in
Sudanese infrastructure, agriculture, and business. He moved
here in 1991 when Turabi had invited him after falling out with
Saudi Arabia's ruling family over their support for the U.S. in
the Gulf War. Turabi believed that with bin Laden's help, Sudan
could spread political Islam globally and jump-start an armed
Islamic revolution. In Sudan, bin Laden had two homes, four
wives (one was Turabi's niece), four sons, and one daughter,
and although he was extremely wealthy, both of his houses were
described as very modest in order to honor his ideals of humble
living.

"Addy, seriously? You can't just go jumping out of moving
cars. You scared the crap out of me."

"How was I supposed to know?"

"It's a picture! All the rickshaws have them!"

"I'm sorry, okay? I can't sleep, I'm sick all the time. The
heat is killing me. I didn't sign up for any of this, you know? I
don't think I can take it anymore."

It was as if she'd stolen the thoughts right out of my head.

\*\*\*

Like mine, Addy's past was riddled with alcohol and drug addiction. She too came to Sudan to sober up and find purpose and meaning in life. But after just two months, we stopped caring. All we could think about was escape, and not the kind that would involve our emergency kits.

"Want to try and find some alcohol? I know some people at the embassy who have a couple crates of beer. They smuggle it in all the time," Addy said.

She didn't have to ask me twice.

"Beer doesn't really count does it? I doubt if we'll even feel a buzz," I said. Of course, I was lying to us both, but Give Me a Vodka Shan was in charge now, and she got a kick out of manipulating the masses.

A few days later our own personal crate arrived and it was the most fantastic thing we'd seen in weeks. The golden, wooden box looked just like a treasure chest you'd find at the bottom of a pirate ship. We busted it open quickly, anxious to see our dazzling gems. My fingers grazed lovingly over the glistening bottles. There were ten of them. No, they were not my precious Vodka, not even close, but they would certainly do.

"Cheers!" I said after we cracked open a few bottles and took long, hearty gulps.

An hour and four beers later, we were drunk and chortling like we'd been best friends for years.

"You be Bashir and I'll be Turabi!" I said. Horrible mockery, I know, but we were two young girls still trying to adjust and find our way in this hard-core escapade, and we'd underestimated how intensely the beer would hit us considering the lack of nutrition and food in our bellies, and the amount of weight we'd lost over the last two months.

"Let's go explore," I suggested. This was a bad idea. It was already dark out.

"What about the curfew?"

"We'll be quick!"

We drank our last beer and headed out. Our first obstacle was to get past our sleeping neighbors. Hovering over them, Addy and I tried hard not to giggle. I saw Jamal, one of our friendly neighbors. He had white hair and only one tooth and the best smile on the block.

"*Marhaba!*" I greeted him with a whisper.

Addy snickered beside me. "Touch him, Shannon. Poke his side."

I poked him and we both howled with laughter. The men stirred and we darted past them so we wouldn't get caught. A little way down the street, I noticed how good it felt to walk without everyone staring at me all the time, and how hard this had been on me. Cloaked in the dark shadows of the night, and in my drunken stupor, I felt free as my feathered friends in the sky. I stuck out my arms.

"WOOHOO," I bellowed out into the night, twirling around like a whirling dervish.

A few weeks ago I'd seen Sudan's dervishes in action at the Hamed al-Nil Tomb in Omdurman. Hundreds had gathered to watch them chant, dance, spin, and clap to hypnotic drumming as the scent of burning frankincense wafted through the air. The dervishes were cloaked in green, red, and white robes and they had *sibha* (Muslim prayer beads) strung loosely around their necks. As the evening went on the dervishes intensified their spellbinding activities several frantic notches while chanting:

"*La illaha illallah.*" *There is no God but Allah.*

Many of the dervishes take a vow of poverty in order to learn humility. Through the endless repetition of chanting and spinning, they go into a trance in order to obtain religious ecstasy in hopes of purifying the soul and finding inner peace.

"Shan, watch out!"

I caught myself with my arms just before I tumbled headfirst into a pothole. Adrenaline surged through my system. My twisted ankle throbbed. It was too dark to see how deep the hole went, but my heart was pounding hard enough to let me know it was a close call.

*"Khawaja!" Foreigner!* a man shouted at us from a bed across the street. "You are drunk? In Sudan? Go home! You are not safe here."

His words killed the party buzz in a matter of seconds. Without making eye contact, Addy and I stopped dead in our tracks, and sighing deeply we headed home. We knew he was right. We weren't safe here, and this was exactly why we were drinking. Neither of us knew how to cope with this dangerous new world that was now our home.

"Well, Toto. I guess it's safe to say we're not in Kansas anymore," I joked.

As soon as I said it, I was struck by something Dr. Reynolds once told me: *Feel your emotions Shannon; don't deflect. Try and breathe into them as they come up and let yourself honor the true self. Emotions can seem scary at times, but they will lose intensity if you stick them out.*

I decided Dr. Reynolds didn't know what he was talking about. He'd never lived in Africa before with Bashir and Turabi or had an Uzi to his head. The memory of his Santa Clause beard and jolly old soul was a startling contrast to our current situation, and I pushed it down angrily.

My joke caused more harm for the both of us than I anticipated. At my side, Addy began to cry softly. Since the policeman had put a gun to her head she cried a lot, and I was never quite sure what to do to soothe her. It was hard to know how to process my own complicated feelings, let alone someone else's. I placed my arm around her shoulder and although it felt awkward, I kept it around her until we got home.

# Chapter 5

*W*aking up with a hangover in Sudan was like waking up in hell.

The water was off and the sun was particularly uncouth. It was so bloody hot that it hurt to move and all we could do was cook in our beds, dehydrated and incapacitated as a couple of baked potatoes. Without running water, the swamp cooler puffed out thick, sizzling air like a fire-breathing dragon, and the fan above my bed whirred obnoxiously—pure torture on my splitting headache. We had no aspirin and only one small bottle of water between us, and neither of us were in any condition to go to the *dukan* (corner shop). I couldn't stop puking, I couldn't brush my teeth, and I couldn't wash off the stench of alcohol exuding from my pores.

In the afternoon, the sun went from nasty to straight-up malicious, and I imagined that the devil himself was standing on top of that great fireball in the sky scoffing with his pitchfork in the air and heavy horns jutting out of his maroon-colored skull.

"Welcome to the underworld, you drunken idiot!" he roared, and then barked out a deep carnivorous laugh that echoed in my mind throughout the day.

A little extreme, but my daydream precisely represented the shame and guilt I felt over my relapse. I couldn't rationalize this one, not without a nice shower, water, and food. So I swore to every God I'd ever heard of that I would never, *ever* drink again if somebody would *please* just transport me to a cool hotel room or at the very least make the pain go away.

The only response I got was from Addy. She'd saunter past my bedroom with her emaciated frame in a yellow tank and a do-rag holding up her afro. Her eyes were bloodshot and there was a white film of saliva on the side of her mouth, and she reminded me of a creature from *Night of the Living Dead*. For once I was grateful there were no mirrors in our home because I'm sure I looked like a zombie too.

"Why is the water off? Today of all days," Addy said on her way to the bathroom.

"Seriously," I grumbled. Even if our shower water was slimy and scalding hot, it was better than nothing.

The one thing we had going for us was that it was Friday, which meant there was no school and we could work through our hangovers in our own time. However, I still had to make a phone call to my dad, which I'd scheduled via email a week ago. I considered walking to the nearest internet café so I could cancel the call via email, but I was too weak to face the outside world. So at the designated hour I lugged myself out of bed and dialed home.

"Hey, Shannon! What's up?" He sounded so casual and cheery.

We chitchatted about the food, weather, and life back in Utah. In my emails home I'd been deliberate about keeping the majority of the chaos out; I wanted them to sleep at night even if I couldn't. But in my vulnerable state I suddenly found that I couldn't hold it in any longer, and I emotionally vomited all over him. I told him about everything: Turabi and the coup, Addy and the curfew, Yusif and the Uzi, and bin Laden and the rickshaw. It was my way of sharing my discomfort without talking about what was bothering me the most: the fact that I'd relapsed.

After I divulged all the frightening details, I waited for my dad to tell me that everything would be okay. But he didn't.

"An Uzi? A coup?" Silence. "Are you sure you don't want to come home?"

"Dad," I began.

"It's okay to come home. Nobody will think less of you. Mom and I can help you figure out your next move."

I couldn't tell him that if I went home now I'd start drinking again and probably wouldn't stop. The environment in Khartoum may not have been ideal, but back home, *I* was an even bigger threat, the number-one variable putting my life at risk. Here at least drinking had proven to be less attractive, and there were no clubs or men to distract with. No ego boosters. The scary truth was that in some twisted way I had a better shot at survival *here*. But how could I explain this to *my father*, a man who had never been addicted before?

"Thanks dad, but I need to stick this out." As soon as I said these words I knew they were true.

We chitchatted a bit more and then my dad sighed. "Well, I've got some bad news, too. We had to put Butterscotch down last night. He took a turn for the worse and we didn't want him to suffer anymore."

Butterscotch? Dead? "Oh, dad." I wept.

Butterscotch had been our family cat since I was thirteen years old. Like insects and kids, animals were another great source of joy for me, and Butterscotch had been a loving and non-judgmental companion during my rocky teen years. He'd cuddle with me all through the night and purr softly in my ear. He always made me feel less alone in the world, and now he was gone.

The tears flowed freely and I was glad for it. Secretly I'd been longing to cry as easily as Addy. I couldn't understand why it was so hard for me, but Butterscotch's death was the catalyst that allowed me to let go and express all the stress I'd been under. For so many years, he'd served my emotional well-being and now he was, in his passing, serving me again.

After I hung up with Dad, I crawled back into bed beneath my insufferable fan and flame-throwing "cooler," and allowed myself to mourn. What else was I going to do? The beer bottles were empty. There were no TVs, no radios, no magazines, and no mirrors. It dawned on me how quickly time was flying by and that I wasn't spending it the way I'd planned. Sure, a lot of terrifying things had happened, but I was alive and I didn't *have to be* the victim of my environment. I could rise above this. Yes, I'd relapsed, but that didn't take away my sober time or the skills I'd enhanced while sober, such as learning to trust my instincts, providing emotional support to a friend, and caring for the needs of a classroom full of smart, vivacious kids. I was becoming less critical of myself and reconnecting with my inner champion. I was learning to be my own friend.

This was encouraging and helped me conclude that it was time to stop merely surviving.

It was time to thrive.

\*\*\*

Bashir rounded up hundreds of Turabi's supporters and the coup ended. I never got any clarity on what happened to the man behind the plan. Was Turabi arrested? Did he flee? Was he hiding out at Yusif's house? Everything was handled in hushed tones. It was as if the guy had just disappeared.

And it was troublesome. The events surrounding the coup had been taxing enough, and now I had to wonder if Turabi was lurking in the shadows planning another revolution. From then on, I never ran on Africa Road again, and I walked around the streets with hypervigilance, especially in the presence of police. Their guns reminded me of Addy's threat and Yusif's Uzi, and it hit too close to home, which provided a window into what it must be like for veterans living with post-traumatic stress disorder. I wore my striped zebra cap whenever I was outdoors because it allowed me to hide my eyes. I could block out the stares, starving and gutted animals, the dust, and everything in between.

In spite of this, I opened myself up to creating a more vivacious life in Khartoum. It was good timing. The weather had started to cool and the city bustled with exciting news: the Second Sudanese Civil war—one of the longest wars on record—was coming to an end after years of marathon negotiations. The Comprehensive Peace Agreement (CPA) would be signed at the beginning of the New Year to signify a permanent ceasefire between the Sudanese government and the Sudan People's Liberation Movement/Army (SPLM/A), a rebel group fighting for the freedoms of all Sudanese and particularly the marginalized southerners. Fighting had broken out between the two parties when the government forcefully tried to impose Sharia on non-Muslim southerners in 1983.

The news of the CPA had created quite a stir on the streets. It was as if a dark tumultuous cloud had lifted: the Sudanese appeared in better spirits, dancing and singing in the middle of the day. It was contagious. In mid-October, Ramadan began. Ramadan is celebrated each year during the ninth month of the Islamic calendar, and all Muslims fast from dawn till dusk, except those suffering from illness and those travelling, pregnant, breastfeeding, diabetic, or menstruating. During Ramadan, Muslims are also required to refrain from smoking and having sex during the day. The time is meant for spiritual reflection, improvement, and increased devotion and worship, and the act of fasting is meant to cleanse the soul by freeing it from impurities. Ramadan also encourages Muslims to empathize with those who are less fortunate, inspiring actions of generosity and giving.

Although children are excluded from the fasting rule, my students were now old enough to fast for one meal each day. They were *so* enthusiastic about this, they couldn't fathom why I was choosing not to fast at all.

"Teacher, please fast with us. At least for lunch!"

"We don't want you to burn in hellfire and damnation, Miss Shannon."

"Yes, teacher! We want you to find Allah!"

*Hellfire and damnation. Allah.* The words were different, but the same. Where had I heard them before? Yes, back home from the mouths of my friends and family. They too had expressed concern for my soul, and here I was, once again, the lost sheep because I was refusing to participate in *someone else's idea* of who God was and what *they thought* God expected of me. I knew my students loved me and were sincerely worried for my well-being. The same went for my family and friends back home. But that didn't mean their perception that I was *lacking,* and therefore in need of *saving,* wasn't damaging. It felt as if I couldn't be viewed as a resource—someone who could contribute substantially to their well-being—because my religious views weren't aligned with theirs. This hurt, a lot.

How was this happening *again*?

There are roughly 7,927 miles, including the Atlantic Ocean, separating Salt Lake City from Khartoum. Yet the similarities between the Mormon and Muslim faith were disconcertingly similar. Both religions were founded by a prophet who received visits from an angel, which lead to the revelation of a book of scripture. Both practice fasting, preach polygamy in the afterlife, and place a very strong emphasis upon chastity, including modest dress (think: garments and the *hijab, niqab,* and *burka*), and both orthodox communities believe that their religion constitutes *the one and only complete and true religion on the earth today.*

It was this last point that struck me most. My students were completely *convinced* that their religion was the one true religion—just like everyone in Utah. I realized how much our environment could play a role in our beliefs, and this helped me realize why I'd always been uncomfortable taking the opinions of others at face value, and why it was important, at least to me, to ask questions and conduct meaningful investigations so I could understand things in a deeper capacity.

"Listen guys, I really appreciate your concern, but let's talk about something else. What should we do for free time today?"

"Why don't you wear a *hijab?*" Saara wanted to know.

"My mom says you are a Mormon because you're from Utah. What's a Mormon?" Ebrahim asked.

"Fasting is not that bad. Your tummy only rumbles for a little while," Yusif swore.

Uncomfortable memories burst into the moment like shaken up champagne and I shivered. I wanted to be open to discussing religion with my students, but I didn't know how. Our relationship was important to me—more important than convincing them of the rightness of my spiritual beliefs. I wondered how I could facilitate a discussion that would honor my own perceptions without putting theirs down or if this were even possible. I felt strongly that using moral absolutism to portray religious ideology, such as "you are morally flawed for disbelieving in this 'fact,'" and then following this up with a threat like "hellfire and damnation in the afterlife" was a dangerous tactic to use on a young mind. I squirmed and thought of the word *brainwashing.* In my life, a religious warning was like having a time bomb planted in my brain at a vulnerable age by the people I trusted most. As I matured, I would have trouble remembering the source of the terrible ticking sound, and then locating it and digging it out.

After being exposed to so much irrationality, it would take years to learn how to think logically. Eventually, I'd be able to rewire my brain and uncover some of the teachings that had confused me as a little girl. For starters, in Holy Books, God was always smiting somebody and yet his followers were expected to turn the other cheek. This hypocrisy reminded me of when my parents would spank me for hitting my sister and yell out, "You are not allowed to hit, you hear me?"

*Huh? Then why are you hitting me?*

Oh, that's right. Because you know better and violence is *bad*. Wait—*what?* Talk about a brain scramble! Luckily, scientific research is proving the significance of parenting due to its effects on the growth and development of a child's brain. Irrational, illogical, inconsistent, and fear-based messaging is literally programmed into a child's brain, altering it so that growth patterns are abnormal and dysfunctional, thus setting the stage for inconsistent, irrational, and fear-based behaviors in the child's future.

Shuffling papers, I dilly-dallied in front of the class. I was in no mood to talk about any of this. I was still feeling raw and vulnerable from my latest relapse even though it had happened nearly two months ago. My Melancholy Posse had duct-taped Peacemaker Shan and stuffed her in their Dungeon of Drudgery, and I was next on their hit list. Since my childhood experiences with religion and God had scarred me so deeply, these topics were huge triggers, and I had to tread lightly. The mere mention of either could cause another relapse, and this would be the case for many years to come—like in 2009, when I got my second DUI, and was court-ordered to attend AA groups. I relapsed anytime I was forced to attend a meeting because the AA program is based on God or spirituality. Nothing wrong with either of these, but *I* associated both with humiliation, rejection, and manipulation. The meetings reminded me of my childhood where an adult authority figure was telling me, rather forcibly, what my relationship with God and myself was supposed to look like. The "Big Book" was even marked up in red like it was a book of scripture and members quoted from it often throughout the meeting. It reminded me of Sunday school and gave me the heebie-jeebies.

"I need a different type of recovery support. Can I do individual counseling instead?" I'd begged the judge who'd ordered me to attend the meetings. It wasn't that I wanted to shun God or AA, but I needed a safe place to process my trauma before throwing myself back into a religious or spiritual setting.

"Absolutely not," the judge said. He knew what he was doing and that was that.

Again an adult authority figure was refusing *my own insight* into decisions that pertained *to my own life*, just as when I was punished for trying to establish a personal relationship with God apart from the Mormon conception. This is what led to my tendency to self-medicate *in the first place*. And being denied the right to self-direct as a struggling alcoholic seeking recovery within the criminal justice system *further exacerbated the original wound*.

Today the Substance Abuse and Mental Health Services Administration (SAMHSA), a branch of the U.S. Department of Health and Human Services, which is charged with improving the quality and availability of prevention, treatment, and rehabilitative services in order to reduce illness, death, disability, and cost to society resulting from substance abuse and mental illnesses, recognizes that every individual's life is unique right down to his or her *trauma experiences*, that these experiences affect and determine an individual's pathway to recovery, and that at the core of each person's recovery path is first and foremost: *the right to self-*

*direct it*. SAMHSA even defines recovery as a "process of change through which individuals improve their health and wellness, live a self-directed life, and strive to reach their full potential."

It's becoming common and critical knowledge that addiction and trauma are closely linked, as many individuals turn to alcohol or drugs to escape from emotional and mental anguish brought on by traumatic experiences. In fact, recent studies have found that between 60 and 90 percent of those struggling with drug or alcohol addiction have experienced at least one major traumatic event in their lifetime.

SAMHSA acknowledges that there are many paths to recovery and that implementing these concepts into American's healthcare and criminal justice systems will lead to a radical transformation of both.

"Teacher? Hello! What are you doing?" Ebrahim said, waving his math test dramatically in the air to get my attention.

"You totally zoned out!" Rashida exclaimed. The kids laughed at me.

Flushed, I realized I was stuck in my childhood again. I clapped my hands together to reorient myself. As I looked out at the kid's curious faces, I wondered if my experiences would always get in the way of our discussions or if I could move past it and be open to the positive aspects of *their* beliefs, no matter how different they were from my own. After all, I'd vowed to remain open while in Sudan and I was learning that true openness meant finding a way to view everyone as a resource. My students could contribute to the expansion of my well-being no matter what their God looked like. Just because Allah didn't speak *my* love language, my students had found incredible value in his teachings, like my family had found incredible value in the Book of Mormon and the Prophet Joseph Smith.

In the future, I'd try and remember this vow whenever I came into contact with someone who had a different recovery path than mine. (By the way, mine is participating in Recovery from Religion support groups, trauma therapy, writing, reading, and meditation.) There are a variety of recovery paths out there including twelve-step groups, SMART Recovery, rehab, LifeRing Secular Recovery, LDS Addiction Recovery, trauma counseling, yoga, nutrition, and many more. However, just as in my Mormon-dominated community, there is a great deal of judgement within the recovery community about which path is the "right" path. I find this incredibly sad and discouraging. Life is tough enough and figuring out how to quit drugs and alcohol can be an excruciating process for individuals who are already demoralized and brokenhearted. Why project our method of recovery onto someone else without considering their personal traumas and goals? Why not open ourselves up to the fact that there are other ways to establish health and well-being? Perhaps there are even multiple ways to connect with God or spirituality or a higher awareness or whatever one prefers to call it or not call it.

Is it possible that everything on Earth has a place and is acting as a conduit to help us connect with metaphysical energy meant to transform the world's perceptions, heal the world's wounds, and open us up to receive our individual power and purpose?

"Okay, class. You want to know what I was thinking about? Alicia Keys! Have you heard her new album yet or what?" Hook, line and sinker—the kids erupted in a passionate discussion about the talented piano player and her stellar new music.

A cop out, I know. But right then I needed space from sensitive issues that I didn't fully understand.

***

Addy and I were in the kitchen chopping vegetables for dinner. Ratatouille was on the menu, Addy's favorite.

"So I got a job working at the *Sudan Vision* as an editor," Addy said. The *Sudan Vision* was one of two independent, daily, English-language newspapers in Khartoum, and Addy's big dream was to become a successful journalist one day. It was the perfect opportunity for her.

"That's cool. How'd you get the job?"

"I just walked in and offered my services. They basically jumped at the chance to hire a native speaker and it made me realize that there's very little competition here. We can pretty much have any job we want."

I hadn't thought about it before, but Addy was right. Since most the foreigners were brought over to work for big, international organizations, and visa restrictions were so tight, there were very few working for Sudanese companies. If we applied ourselves, we could probably work in any capacity we wanted.

I sliced into a tomato and its guts exploded; I licked the tasty juice off my fingers.

"The pay is pretty good, too. The *Sudan Vision* isn't in need of another editor, but maybe you could apply at the *Khartoum Monitor* doing the same thing." The *Khartoum Monitor* was the second independent daily, and the two papers were competitors — both referring to themselves as the "leading daily in Khartoum."

"Dude, I'm not a writer and I don't know anything about politics or Sudan."

"Didn't you tell me that you used to write books as a teenager?"

"Those were just short stories. I never shared them with anybody."

Addy gave me a sideways glance. "What about your journal? You write in that thing all the time."

Another good point. And not only did I write *a lot*, but I did *love* to write. It was a skill that came naturally to me. Plus, I enjoyed researching and learning about the world. What better place to do all these things at once (while getting paid) than at a newspaper agency in Khartoum?

A few days later, I went to the *Khartoum Monitor* to ask for a job. Surprisingly, it was located close to our neighborhood, but the building wasn't flashy, so I'd failed to notice it. As I approached the door, my heart fluttered. I was impressed that I'd even dared to show up. Who knew what opportunities would come if they hired me?

Inside the *KM* were a handful of southern Sudanese men and woman typing enthusiastically on a row of ancient computers. Towering over them was a lanky man with thick bifocal lenses and black rims. He had his arms folded across his chest and it looked as if he were giving important instructions. I assumed he was the man in charge, and since I had nothing to lose, I walked up to him, held out my hand, and told him I was looking for a job as an editor.

His name was William Ezekiel and he was the editor-in-chief. William gave me a long, curious look, and motioned for me to come in and have a seat. "We are blessed to have you come at this particular time. You know there are many things happening in Sudan and we are up to our heads with information that must always go out tomorrow."

He motioned for me to sit in a chair near his desk and after we were both seated, he told me that the *KM* worked to "ensure the rights of all Sudanese people with special regard to the people of Southern Sudan, Southern Blue Nile, Abyei, and the Nuba Mountain regions. Since these populations were highly marginalized, they need a strong and powerful voice fighting for them." Abyei, the Nuba Mountains, and the Blue Nile are transitional and contested areas since they straddle the north-south political, military, and cultural fault lines.

"But the first objective of this newspaper is peace. We challenge *both* the Sudanese government and the SPLM/A by publishing what we actually see and hear on the ground, and this has gotten us into trouble many times."

"What kind of trouble?"

He shrugged, "We've been shut down six, maybe seven times this year. But we always come back."

He wasn't joking. Seven months from then, William would receive a letter from Sudan's Press Council stating the Supreme Court had decided to revoke the *Khartoum Monitor*'s license while it reviewed a 2003 court case, which found the newspaper guilty of crimes against the state for publishing a story about slavery in southern Sudan. The *KM* would lose its license for over a month, but as William had stated, they would come back.

"We only have one hour before deadline and I need you to edit two articles." He sat me down in front of a computer, uploaded a few files, and began to point at the screen.

"Here, these two need a bit of work. Can you get to them right away?"

I beamed. "Does this mean I have the job?"

William nodded.

I couldn't believe it. I was working for a Sudanese newspaper. I felt so official. But it quickly faded once I skimmed over the articles. One discussed the continuing violence in Darfur, which was derailing attempts to solve the genocide, and the other highlighted the deaths of two Sudanese who were working for Save the Children UK and were killed by the *Janjaweed* while traveling in a humanitarian convoy in South Darfur. The English was dreadful in both. I'd have to do a complete rewrite in order to make sense of things. So I did.

The next day I picked up a copy of the *KM* on my way to school and saw that none of my edits had been included. Both articles were in their original format. I asked William about it that night and all he had to say was:

"Maybe do a lighter edit next time?"

Over time I learned that a "lighter edit" meant changing five to eight words, but definitely no more than ten. This was because the Sudanese put a lot of effort and pride into their work. I think they thought my changes tainted their original message and, frankly, I respected that. I got paid just the same, and the job allowed me to learn about Sudan and share in exciting news with the locals as things came up. I started to identify with the problems as a fellow human—not an outsider—and understand how they affected the world as a whole. Our work at the paper became personal. I too wanted peace, even if I didn't know how we'd obtain it.

*Shwaya, shwaya,* my body adjusted to the harsh environment and I could enjoy the Sudanese *shai, tamia,* and *ful* without getting sick. I could play basketball in the heat with the kids without passing out or getting dizzy. I bought more modest clothes with the money I earned from the *KM* and found ways to blend in.

Christmas came and went without a single snowflake, carol, or over-the-top Target commercial, and I hardly noticed. During the first week of the New Year, William dropped a piece of paper on my desk. It was a Reuters article entitled "Sudan Set for Peace Next Week!" Over the last several months, the Sudanese government and SPLM/A had been working hard to iron out issues relating to the peace process, such as how to roll out democratic governance throughout the country and share oil revenues equitably. The signing of the CPA would kick off a six-year interim period that would precede a referendum to determine whether the south would remain joined with the north.

"Can you believe it? In just a couple days' time it will be a done deal. No more forced Sharia on our Christian people. I'm proud to say the CPA was partially brought about by our staff here. We pressed on for peace, we paid our dues. Now it's finally here!"

William jumped up and down like a schoolboy and it was hard not to get caught up in his enthusiasm, but I had a funny feeling in my gut. Even though I really wanted the peace process to go smoothly for all of us, I knew from personal experience that deep-seated issues, especially those pertaining to religion, took years of hard work to target and then years more to figure out the exact damage that had been done so peace could finally be obtained. The way the Sudanese were talking on the streets, it was like they expected the CPA to magically heal decades of resentments and misunderstanding overnight.

I wasn't putting my money on it.

# Chapter 6

It was Sunday, January 9th, 2005, and one of the most significant days in Sudan's history.

Leaders from around the world had gathered in Nairobi, Kenya, to witness the official signing of the Comprehensive Peace Agreement (CPA) between the Sudanese government and the Sudan People's Liberation Movement/Army (SPLM/A). The United Nations Secretary-General, Kofi Annan, applauded this move and in a statement he commended "the dedication of the Sudanese delegates, who persevered to bring the talks to a successful conclusion."

One major Sudanese delegate—and the single most influential person in the implementation of the CPA—was Dr. John Garang. Garang had established the SPLM/A rebel militia in order to fight for a "New Sudan," which included opposing military rule and Islamic dominance in the country. This action brought about Sudan's Second Civil War, a conflict that killed at least two million, uprooted four million, and forced nearly 600,000 individuals to take refuge in neighboring countries. But the tragedy also led to the independence of the southern Sudanese.

Thus the southerners adored him. In their eyes, Garang was a hero. He was the one person with enough guts to rally the suppressed minorities and form a majority that could one day rule. His goal was to empower his Christian people, and then together with the northerners, replace President Bashir with a government made up of representatives from "all tribes and religions in Sudan."

"The agreement belongs to every Sudanese, to all of you," he said. "Our house has many rooms...there is a place for everyone." There are hundreds of tribes in Sudan, including the Jamala and the Nubians in the north, the Beja near the Red Sea, and several Nilotic tribes down south, such as the Azande, Dinka, Nuer, and Shilluk. Beside Islam (the majority of the Muslims in Sudan are Sunni), there are a variety of religious communities, too, including traditional indigenous religions, Roman Catholics, Greek Orthodox, Coptic Christians, and Anglicans.

The CPA represented Garang's "New Sudan" in that it required the current government to rewrite the constitution so that Islamic law no longer applied to non-Muslims in the country. It would also allow Christians to hold high-status positions within the government—positions no Christian or southerner had ever held, and Garang himself was set to be inaugurated as the second Vice President in July.

Once the news broke that the CPA was a done deal, the Sudanese exploded onto the streets in a state of heightened euphoria. They danced, screamed, sang, laughed, and cried, and for some it was all of these things at once. I was caught off guard by this passionate display because of how raw and uninhibited it was. They sobbed so that their entire bodies shook, as if the war had been trapped inside them, and now that peace was here, they could release it.

The southern Sudanese were *finally* free.

Their elation lasted a day, maybe two. By Tuesday, the energy in Khartoum had shifted from divine ecstasy to nervous anticipation. Distrust was everywhere. It swept through the streets like a deadly airborne disease, infecting anyone who breathed. The citizens were like children who'd grown up with physically abusive parents: even though their abusers now had their hands tied behind their backs, they were still shielding their head with their fists in anticipation of the blow.

Which came quickly.

The first point of confrontation was that Garang wasn't everyone's cup of tea. He was known for having a massive ego and he had zero tolerance for anyone who disagreed with him, even his followers. The punishment for those who did? Prison or death.

Another issue was that Garang's rebel army had been accused of human rights abuses, which included mass killings and rapes, widespread torture, unwarranted incarcerations, and kidnappings. (Ten years later, in 2014, the leadership of the SPLM/A would publicly admit to all these things.) Needless to say, there were many people who despised the rebel militia and many more who wanted Garang dead.

Also, since the provisions of the CPA were specific to the north-south conflict, it wouldn't cover the catastrophe in Darfur, which was deteriorating with each passing day. Attacks on innocent civilians (the majority women and children) by the *Janjaweed,* a government-backed militia, were happening more frequently. Everybody was a target, even national and international aid workers. The United Nations hadn't yet concluded that genocide was taking place in Darfur although it had confirmed that mass killings were occurring, possibly even a few "genocidal acts." Regardless, many worried that if the government was supplying this militia with guns and planes to conduct such cruelty...how serious could it really be about peace? The international community hoped the CPA would provide a template for a solution to this conflict too, but most felt that the instability in the west would have a negative effect on the fragile peace in other areas.

Pretty soon, the media confirmed it: Sudan was in crisis. Again. The UN issued a warning that peace needed to be a priority, and reminded the Sudanese that the Captain of Peacemaking himself (take note of my sarcasm), Omar al-Bashir, had recently stated:

"We call upon all the sons of Sudan, inside and outside, to embrace peace—to listen to the voice of wisdom and to give priority to dialogue by making it the only path to solving our problems."

But Sudan would continue to constitute a threat to both national and international peace and security, and in March 2005, the UN Security Council established the United Nations Mission in the Sudan (UNMIS), which was tasked with supporting the implementation of the CPA, humanitarian assistance, protection, and promotion of human rights.

While working at the *Khartoum Monitor*, I'd become more aware of the media and the critical role it played in any given situation. I knew from personal connections that the Sudanese were highly intelligent and deep thinkers. They read the news daily and would sit outside at dusk and discuss the political, geographical, and economic situations of not just Sudan, but other countries around the world. They were passionate about figuring out a way to solve the issues of their country and they trusted the media to lead the way.

As the news continued to highlight the growing instability (one headline I read: *Sudan, peace? What peace?*) I watched it create tension on the streets and burn bridges between neighbors. It reminded me of *The Truman Show*, a movie starring Jim Carrey about the life of Truman Burbank, who is initially unaware that he is living in a constructed reality TV show packed with commercials and paid actors, which is broadcast 24/7 to billions of people throughout the world. The Sudanese were like Truman:

they were being watched by hundreds of communities, national and international. Their every move was broadcast to the world, fodder for the media machine's flashy stories that spawned innumerable paid ads and commercials. They had no idea they were being exploited. It was the greatest show on Earth and they were its subject—*coming to you live every day!*

I had to wonder if there were better ways to discuss a crisis without contributing to it. I puzzled over my role in all of this. Didn't negative media attention increase negativity, and positive attention improve peace? It wasn't about pointing fingers—I was starting to get to know many of the journalists working for companies like Reuters, CNN, BBC and *Al Jazeera*, and they were good, hardworking people. But something was off. It seemed the media had forgotten the bigger purpose for being in Sudan and reporting the stories of those who lived there. Perhaps they too were seeking a new way but were stuck in the past, bumping up against old walls.

If only there were a way to bring light to an issue without casting a shadow over it or the people involved. Was that even possible? Maybe the key was simply focusing on the peace-building that was happening around the country—even if it was only in two percent.

This was a critical point for me to try and understand, and then put into practice—but at times I too would forget about the bigger picture.

The media machine was well-oiled and it would suck me right in.

\*\*\*

A few weeks after the signing of the CPA, I went to Afra, Sudan's first shopping mall, which opened a year before I got there and was located in Arkawet, a suburb of Khartoum. Afra

Mall had fully functioning air conditioning (*Alhamdullilah!*), a few movie theatres, and proper department stores. I'd discovered it by accident and when I did I was a) super annoyed that Fifi had never mentioned it, and b) blown away by how Westernized it was. Not only did it have a massage parlor and beauty salon, but there were *escalators*.

I ordered kofta in the food court and while looking for a spot to eat, I saw Samson, the UN Children's Fund (UNICEF)'s project officer of peace-building. He was enjoying a bowl of Asian cuisine. Sitting beside him was Doodee, a volunteer for Peace Culture Project (PCP) of Sudan University, a UNICEF-supported project established to introduce peace-building skills into rural communities. I'd met both men at a recent press conference I had started to attend regularly in order to be "in the know" and enhance my community relationships.

"*Fudul*," Samson said. *Welcome.* Samson was your typical kindhearted Sudanese. He greeted me with an enthusiastic smile and handshake.

I grinned, happy to see him. I always enjoyed talking with him. Bright and captivating, he reminded me of William. He looked like William, too, with his thick glasses and dark leathery skin. Doodee, a man of the Ngok Dinka tribe, used to live in Abyei, a town that had been a major battle ground during the civil war.

When I initially met Doodee he told me that growing up he'd had no food, water, or medical care. If you fell ill in his village, you died. But despite his harrowing past, Doodee radiated optimism and triumph. He had a baby face, like me, and he lit up when he talked about his schooling and volunteer work. He had moved to Khartoum in search of a better life and he believed that through education and service work he could make a difference in his country.

"So tell me a little bit more about the peace projects you're working on," I said, my mouth full of lamb. A chunk fell out on my plate and without skipping a beat, I stabbed it with my fork and shoved it back in.

Samson scooped a pile of rice and sautéed vegetables into his mouth, chewed ravenously, and then swallowed. "Now that the displaced people are heading back to their villages, we've run into some interesting, new problems."

Samson explained that there was little support and infrastructure for the thousands of people who'd been displaced by the war and were returning home spontaneously, as well as for the thousands more that were expected to return in the coming months.

"There could be fights over rehabilitation of villages, distribution of school supplies, and local power. It is sure to be a catastrophe. Communities have been divided for years resulting in the multiplication of leaders of the same tribe. New chiefs will be heading back to their villages, and they will claim to be the real chief. This is why the PCP's peace-building projects are crucial for helping with this transition."

As he shoveled in another bite of rice and vegetables, I stabbed at a succulent piece of lamb. Doodee, who'd been relishing a plate of stuffed dolmas and fish, perked up.

"Our projects focus on building healthy relationships between communities that have typically been at war. We create a platform where the communities can get education about their rights and learn how to claim them without using force."

I wiped my mouth with a napkin and gulped down a glass of cold soda. This sounded like exactly what the Sudanese needed. I asked what their process involved.

"Our volunteers travel to places of conflict and use traditional songs and dance about killing and fighting and make them about peace. The new messages suggest ways for communities to

resolve their differences. I hope one day to return to my village and teach the members of my tribe how to resolve their conflicts without fighting. I will tell all the young people there that we must learn to grow together and respect one another so we can live in one area together in harmony."

"I am optimistic that with time people will embrace peace," Samson said. "But for now, peace is only on paper. We have a very long, hard road ahead of us."

Later that night, at the *KM*, I walked in excited to tell William about my conversation with Samson and Doodee. I began to look forward to sharing everything I learned with William. He would listen with great intent and his eyes would twinkle. "See! You are getting it!" It made me feel good.

"You know what I think?" William said. "I think you should write your own column."

"What would I write about?"

"You could offer an American's view on the various issues in Sudan. What insight can you, as an outsider, offer the Sudanese that might be helpful to us? We are all so close to the problems here. Sometimes it is very hard for us to see our way out."

I was touched. He had provided me with an opportunity to expand my understanding of his people. His actions told me that he really wanted me to thrive, and now that I was beginning to, in some small way, *know* the Sudanese, I found myself genuinely wanting them to thrive too. We were on this planet together after all. What happened here affected the rest of the world even if we couldn't see it outright.

"*Naaam, shukran,*" I said. *Yes, thank you.*

"*Aafwan,*" William said. *You're welcome.*

\*\*\*

For history class, my students chose to study Sudanese politics. They were fascinated by the CPA and the conflict surrounding it. It was tough at first to break things down into simple terms so they could understand, but eventually I got the hang of it. One day we were discussing a clause of the CPA that gave the south autonomy for six years followed by a referendum of independence in 2011.

"What's auto-no-money?" Rashida asked.

"It's not autonomoney," Saara scolded. Then she looked doubtful. "Right, teacher?"

I smiled. "Right, Saara. You spell it: A-U-T-O-N-O-M-Y." I wrote it out on the chalkboard. "It means to self-govern. So the south is now a self-governing community and will remain that way over the next six years followed by a referendum on independence in the year 2011."

"What does this word mean, 'self-governing?'" Fatima piped up.

This topic had been on my mind a lot lately. "It means that the southerners will be allowed to make decisions based on their own perceptions, desires, and goals. For instance, they can now practice Christianity without being harassed by police."

I spelled another word on the chalkboard. "Does anybody know what referendum means?"

Dalila crinkled her nose. Mohammed yawned. Yusif looked straight-up confused. Behind them was our large classroom window and through it the sun cast fire-orange beams across the kids' faces. As usual, we were cramped in our quarters and being heated like a pack of chicken nuggets in a cheap Kenmore microwave. Still, it was a lovely day.

"Referendum is a type of event where people will vote on a specific issue. The issue that will be voted on in 2011 will be on whether or not Sudan will remain one whole country, consisting of the northern and southern people, or to split the country in half."

"Cut Sudan in half?" Mohammed gasped.

"But if they cut Sudan in half it will be sloppy and broke!" Joseph exclaimed.

"Why can't everyone just cheer up? We just ended a war," Dalila said.

"It's not so bad, really. It's kind of like a divorce where two people who tried really hard to make a relationship work decide that they can't, so they break up."

The kid's eyeballs popped out of their heads. I thought of Addy and her *Beetlejuice* look.

"Teacher! My parents said divorce is a very bad thing and that married people should always try and work it out," Saara said.

I made a face. *Oops.*

I forgot that although divorce is permitted in Islam, it is not encouraged. While the divorce process is easy for men (by the traditional terms of *"talaq,"* a man has to notify his wife three times that he is divorcing her, and after he says this the third time, the divorce is final) it is a very long and challenging process for a woman.

I chewed on my bottom lip. I had gotten an idea for my first column.

I would have the students write short letters to Sudan from their perception and call it "insight from the innocent." But first, they'd need a little more coaching. I thought of a method of communication called Nonviolent Communication, which I'd stumbled upon while cruising the internet for ideas for my first column. Nonviolent Communication was a process developed by Marshall Rosenberg in the 1960s and focused on self-empathy, empathy for others, and honest self-expression. The overall intention was to inspire compassion in others while expressing individual needs and making specific requests to meet those needs.

Rosenberg had initiated peace programs in war-torn areas throughout the world, including Rwanda, Burundi, Nigeria, Malaysia, Indonesia, and the Middle East. He believed that all human beings had the capacity for compassion and only resorted to violence or passive aggressive communication, a form of psychological violence, when they lacked effective strategies for meeting their needs. Since all human needs are universal they're never in conflict with one another. Therefore, conflict only arises when the *strategies* for meeting needs clashed. Rosenberg concluded that if individuals could figure out a way to identify their needs and express them while identifying with the needs of others, harmony would prevail. He believed that one major type of life-alienating communication is the use of "moralistic judgments that imply wrongness or badness on the part of people who don't act in harmony with our values."

"One of the main reasons for the fighting is that the southerners and northerners both think that their ideas, beliefs, and traditions are good and right. In the eyes of the southerners, you—" I pointed at most everyone in the class. Joseph was the only Christian. "—are *wrong* for fasting during Ramadan because they think Allah is *bad*."

"But," I continued, "when we think this way toward another human being, it creates a big, brick wall separating us from them. This isn't helpful to anyone since we're all on this planet together, and even though we appear different, we have the same needs and goals. Can you think of one goal you might have in common with the southerners?"

"To be happy," Dalila said.

"To be rich," Ebrahim added.

"Yes, everyone wants to be happy and to be able to afford things that will enhance their lives."

"But Miss Shannon, what if the southerners call us stupid for fasting or hit us because we pray to Allah?" Yusif asked.

"Those are really good questions, Yusif. When people are being mean to me, I like to imagine what kind of pain they experienced in their life. From what you know of the war, you know that the southerners suffered a lot, right?"

"We all suffered," Saara pointed out.

"Yes, exactly. Do you see? The war and all the suffering that came with it, that is something you have in common with each other. So if they treat you badly, try to remember that their suffering is similar to your suffering and it will help your heart go soft."

"But one boy—he hit me and called me stupid for wearing this," Yusif pointed at the turban on his head. "So I hit him back."

"Well, I read in the newspaper recently that a little southern boy watched his dad get murdered with a machete and then he was forced to leave his family and fight in the war. Do you think that maybe this boy who hit you had something similar like that happen to him? And if so, do you think it would be hard to lose your dad like that? Would it make you angry and maybe even want to hit somebody?"

The kids nodded their heads eagerly. They got it, and I felt they were now ready to hear about our class project for the *KM*. When I explained it they were beyond excited. The kids suggested drawing a cheery picture to go with their letters, and I thought of Doodee' peace projects, and the PCP's use of creativity to build bridges.

"You guys have the best ideas ever," I applauded them.

After recess, they began writing their letters to Sudan and as I walked around the room to glance at their work, this is what I read:

> *Twenty-one years there was a war in South Sudan. They done the war, they stop it. They said, "Let's make a CPA." Okay, then they make friends. In Darfur there is a war again. Let's go there and make friends too. From, Yusif*

*Dear Sudan, We know that you are having a fight so please stop this killing fight. Live happy. Do you want to cut Sudan in half? That is a crazy way! You have 6 years to think, so think good. From Dalila*

*Dear Sudan, We want to help all people of Sudan, southerners and northerners, because we love Sudan. We want all to be friends. We should help the one that does not have anything. From, Fatima*

*Dear Sudan, Stop fighting! You are friends! Don't think that they are bad and don't cut Sudan in half. It is all our country! We are all friends! We are black and they are black so don't think that they are different. We are like them so don't think that they are bad and we are good. Good Luck! From, Ebrahim*

In July 2011, after an overwhelming number of southern Sudanese voted to separate from the north, South Sudan claimed its independence and became Africa's newest country since Eritrea split from Ethiopia in 1993.

***

Back home that evening after I had finished up the article, I burst into Addy's room. She was busy typing on her laptop.

"I'm almost done with my first article. Want to read it?" I asked.

Addy barely glanced at me. "Not really," she mumbled.

She'd been acting cold and distant toward me ever since I told her about William's offer, and it marked the beginning of the end of our friendship. She seemed jealous, although I didn't know why because Addy had recently started her own column at the *Sudan Vision*. Maybe she thought I was trying to steal her thunder? After our time in Sudan, I reached out to her via email to try and mend whatever had broken between us. When I mentioned the rift, her response was that she thought we fell apart because we were working for a "very shady organization [BES] in a very shady country and things were hard."

I wished we could've worked things out while in Sudan because our life paths were headed in similar directions. We both suffered from addiction and not knowing our worth or place in the world. I appreciated the person she was trying to become; Addy was the catalyst that led me to my writing career.

My first article ran in the paper one week later, and even though Addy didn't comment on it, the kids were thrilled.

\*\*\*

But my life was about to change dramatically again, and there was no way I could've seen the direction it would take, not even in my wildest dreams. All thanks to Reuters correspondent Farah Jones.

Farah was the quintessential dream girl. She struck me as a combination of Wonder Woman's Lynda Carter, with drop dead gorgeous looks and *to die for* accessories, and Amal Alamuddin, the ultra-intelligent London-based Lebanese-British lawyer, activist, and author, who specialized in international law, criminal law, and human rights.

In Sudan, Farah was at the top of the expat food chain, a woman with immense power. In 2002, she joined Reuters, an international news agency headquartered in London, and in 2003, she moved to Cairo to cover news for Egypt and Sudan. Eventually, Reuters asked Farah to establish its first bureau in Sudan since the news service vacated the country fifteen years prior. Today, the bureau consists of two full-time journalists, two TV crews, and a stringer—all thanks to Farah. She also had her own Wikipedia page and was incredibly kind.

Eventually Farah was stationed in Khartoum. I met her at a press conference where Jan Pronk, a Dutch politician and the UN Special Representative for Sudan, addressed the media about the uprising in Darfur. From then on, I saw Farah at various expat events throughout Khartoum and we became acquaintances.

One day, I ran into her at the grocery store. Even shopping, I found it hard not to stare at her with my mouth open. She was *that* beautiful.

"Hi, Shannon! How are you, darling?"

I could hardly believe she remembered my name, let alone that she thought I was a darling.

We exchanged small talk and then Farah said, "Have you heard? The UN is looking for a stringer." Stringer is another term for 'freelance journalist.'

"Oh, really," I said, unsure where this was going.

She flashed a spectacular, heartfelt smile, and I fidgeted beside myself. She was so influential and talented and yet she seemed to have no troublesome ego. And here I was, a struggling alcoholic who had no right even being here considering I was a simple girl from Utah with little education and travel experience—at least this was what my Melancholy Posse liked to whisper or shout at me. Farah's ability to make space for me without feeling threatened was a skill I hoped to develop. No doubt, it was one of those tools for maintaining a healthy, happy life.

"Have you thought of applying for the position?"

I stammered. I couldn't figure out why she had suggested this. I'd only written a few articles for the *KM* at this point

"You've got a gut for this stuff and you're *here* in *Khartoum*. *Carpe diem,* darling."

Wow. She was both Mother Teresa *and* Lynda Carter, a very cool combination. I vowed that one day I would figure out how to be just like her: secure, supportive, a bright, encouraging light for all women seeking to step into their authentic power.

I sat on the lead for a couple of days trying to figure out what to do. School was ending soon. In a few months I'd head home. Had I accomplished all I set out to achieve? If I applied for this job, I'd have to teach again in order to renew my work visa, which meant I'd have to commit to another year. I'd heard there were better international schools to work for all over Khartoum, so I could branch out and try something new…but what would my parents say?

As I weighed the pros and cons I felt like I was floating on my back in the ocean and looking up at the twinkling night sky. I could feel in every molecule of my body a massive tide coming in—and I felt no fear. Instead, I was inspired to *let go* and enjoy the thrill of being lifted up by the waves. And then, if I could remember to remain calm as the wave descended toward the earth, I'd make it all the way to the beach, safely, and have experienced this: the joy of being alive.

I applied for the stringer position with the Integrated Regional Information Networks (IRIN), an award-winning humanitarian news and analysis service of the United Nations Office for the Coordination of Humanitarian Affairs. IRIN wanted writing samples so I sent what I had and it was enough to land the job. They sent over a contract that indicated the pay was pretty awful and I wouldn't get a byline (but I would get credit for photos!) because once I sold stories to IRIN, they would be the property of the UN. But what did I care?

I'd be reporting on behalf of the Sudanese for the *United freaking Nations*.

I jumped up from my seat at the BES teacher lounge to do a victory dance. It was after hours and I was all alone. In a bizarre turn of events, my Melancholy Posse showed up and they were all decked out in fluorescent yellow cheerleading outfits with the words GO SHAN sprawled across their backs in white print.

"Dude, this is awesome! You're going to be a ROCK STAR!" Doubting Shan said.

"This is the most exciting thing that's ever happened to us. *Mabrook*! Congrats!" Punk Shan said, her pom pom high in the air like Liberty's torch. Before I could respond, they burst into a cheer which went like this:

"Shan, Shan, she's our clan, if she can do it, anyone can! Gooooooo Shan!"

I rolled my eyes, trying hard to look annoyed. Not only were these fools suddenly speaking in Arabic, but Peacemaker Shan had obviously been working her charms over them. "Oh, I get it. Now that I have a cool new job you're suddenly my biggest fans, huh?"

I guess it's a pretty standard scenario for most of us. We can be entirely supportive of ourselves when things are going well, but critical and mean when they're not. I hoped one day, for the sake of myself and my Melancholy Posse, we could learn to be loving in both the good times *and* the bad. I didn't only need this in order to thrive; I deserved it.

# Chapter 7

*I*n my hand I held a plane ticket to Kenya and a piece of paper with the words "exit visa requested for United Nations Mission" written on it.

Um, yeah. This *really* happened and it was kind of a *big deal*.

Though I'd chosen Sudan, Kenya was really the Africa of my childhood dreams. Its capital city, Nairobi, was known as the "green city in the sun" and the "safari capital of the world." Both of these descriptions summed up my fantasy perfectly: lush jungles and exotic animals.

The exit slip was a big deal because (unbeknown to me) leaving Khartoum was an extremely difficult process without signed documentation from a legitimate organization. I would find this out a little later down the road when I wanted to leave on my own accord. For now all I knew was that I had an invite from IRIN (Integrated Regional Information Networks) to attend a media training along with other IRIN stringers working in the Horn of Africa and nearby areas, which included Eritrea, Djibouti, Ethiopia, Somalia, Sudan, Kenya, the Dominican Republic of Congo, and Uganda. The trip expenses were fully covered: hotel, flight, and a comfortable stipend for food and souvenirs. My new boss, Erich, IRIN's editor-in-chief for the Horn of Africa, mentioned that the trip would also include a safari adventure at Nairobi National Park. It seemed I'd get to live out my jungle-explorer dreams after all.

"I'm going to Kenya!" I jumped up and down in my bedroom like a schoolgirl—minus the pigtails—squealing with delight.

But the trip was still weeks away and in the meantime I had a lot to figure out and quickly. Ever since I'd signed on with IRIN, Erich had been relentless via email:

*Did you get the story about the flare-ups of gender-based violence in Darfur? And the tribal dispute in the Nuba Mountains?*

The truth was that I didn't know how to go about gathering information to write a news story for IRIN, but I couldn't necessarily tell him that. So I responded with:

*No, sorry! I'm still trying to get set up. I'll get the next one!*

There was so much I didn't know about being a journalist in Sudan at that time. In order to write a hot news story, which is basically a short story about a crisis situation happening in real time, you have to have everything at your fingertips: an extensive contact list, good community relationships, a strong internet connection, a translator, and a car. If you didn't have these things when you needed them and it delayed your story as a result, the piece would be tossed into the virtual trash. That's hot news: it's *now*.

I found myself wishing (and I know this is terrible) that the instability would kick back up in Khartoum, at least a tiny bit, so I could get Erich off my back.

But the *news* was occurring clear down south in Juba or in the Nuba Mountains of South Kordofan or west in Darfur. Even if I had everything I needed—including a crisis in Khartoum—it wasn't as if I could run around and cover the news all day. I still had a full-time job teaching.

The situation felt like one of those puzzles without any missing pieces, and all I had to do was relax and let it sort itself out. Farah's angelic face kept popping up in my mind. Since I'd landed the job I'd seen her around town a few times. She'd been happy for me: "If you have any questions or need any help getting started, give me a call."

I didn't want to bother her so I never did, but the clock was ticking and Erich was getting more impatient.

He emailed one Thursday morning: *Shannon, what are you doing over there? Where is the news?*

As soon as school ended that day, I called Farah. "Why don't you come over?" she said. "There's a story unfolding right now. The government's security team is forcibly relocating IDPs in a squatter area called Soba Eradi."

IDP stands for "internally displaced persons" and refers to someone who is forced to flee their home but remains within the borders of their country.

I couldn't believe my luck, but Farah laughed this off. "There's always a story going on somewhere in Sudan."

She gave me her address and I grabbed my notepad and purse. I was nearly out the door when I noticed Addy's silhouette through her bedroom doorway. She was sitting on her bed and I could hear her fingers pitter-pattering away on the keyboard. She was probably trying to secure her big break—like me. I had heard through the grapevine that she'd landed a job doing freelance broadcasting for Voices of America, which meant her stories would be broadcast over the radio and in her own voice as opposed to through the written word like mine. But she too was experiencing difficulty producing an actual story due to lack of resources and time. We were so similar.

I knew we were both better off *helping one another*. But she'd completely shut me out and I still had no idea why. The harder I tried to get close to her and fix the situation, the harder she pulled away. This hurt me because she was the only person in Sudan who really understood what I was going through. I had opened up to her about my struggles with addiction and my strict religious upbringing. I missed our late-night chats and hookah sessions. I didn't want to have to figure out Sudan on my own. I felt lonely without her by my side.

As I stared at her shadow on the wall, I considered saying: *why'd you pull away, Addy? Did I do something wrong?* But I never worked up the courage to ask her outright.

Instead, I stood silently and debated over what to do. I could invite Addy to Farah's or I could leave her here twiddling her thumbs. I imagined her sitting alone and a twisted Grinchy smile spread over my face. I liked the idea of leaving her here because I was so angry with her—or perhaps more accurately, I'd been sideswiped and wounded by her sudden cold shoulder. Not inviting her to Farah's, and right as I got my big break and moved along with my career, would be the best payback ever.

*Take your rejection, Addy, and shove it!*

But the idea of moving forward without her didn't feel right. Even if we couldn't be friends, we were still two women fighting for the same cause: to overcome our issues and step into our unique power and purpose. And isn't that what I'd adored so much about Farah? She had been able to extend her power and resources to me without a bat of her silky-smooth eyelashes, and because of her I now had a ticket to Kenya and would not only play with the hippos and alligators, but *I was going to write for the UN*.

I moved toward Addy's door and opened my mouth but my voice caught in the back of my throat. Painful emotions swelled in my heart, and like a geyser, they wanted to erupt. I wanted her to hurt like I did, but then I thought of Addy and her big dreams. I knew a thing or two about dreams and how hard it was to pursue them in this cynical, jaded world, especially in a place like Sudan. She was a Fearless Warrior Princess in her own right.

I cleared my throat and peeked my head through her door.

"Hey, Farah invited me over to her house to cover the IDP situation in Soba Eradi. Do you want to come? She said I could use her press list and I'm sure she'd let you borrow it, too."

Addy looked up; her eyes flickered with hope. She grabbed her book bag.

On the ride over we made small talk, but the wall between us was like the Berlin—twelve feet high, four feet thick, and constructed of reinforced concrete. Our relationship would get ugly and then really ugly, but I'll spare you the theatrical details. The lesson for me wasn't in this drama, but in understanding why our friendship ended. In 2015, I reached out to Addy again but this time on Facebook, and I sent her a message to see if we could chat. I told her I was writing a book. I wanted her input so I could include her side of the story. She wrote back that she was afraid of what I might say about her. She worried I might portray her in a way that would jeopardize her reputation and career, and she wanted to get her lawyers involved.

*That isn't my intention. I wish you no harm. I've been thinking about you and wondered if we could talk?* I wrote.

All I really wanted was to understand the situation better so I could know my part in it. I used to be convinced that it was all Addy's fault, yet after I hit the rock bottom of my own life and career, I began to see myself a little more clearly—and what I saw was how deeply flawed and self-centered I could be. I know now that I have the tendency to be cruel, manipulative, and egotistical.

In order to give up drinking for good, I had to be willing to look at myself as part of the problem—in *every* situation of my life. Addy's perception of what happened would be extremely valuable for my growth. Like a light, it would shine on the splintered aspects of my soul and personality, and if I could remain open to her feedback and honor my work, I could heal and transform these aspects. But the sad news is that Addy never took me up on my request, and so I still only know my side of the story.

Back in Khartoum, we drifted apart mentally but not physically. Like two ships, we sailed along the same current for years. She ended up staying in Sudan to work as a stringer and then moved on to other countries and publications. She went on to do some incredibly cool and important work, but I can't share those details because I promised to protect her identity.

"Here you be," the cab said in broken English. We were at Farah's gorgeous home in the center of Khartoum. She opened her door and said, "Come on in!" She was on the phone and was covering the mouthpiece with her hand.

Speaking into her phone she said, "Yes, yes, thank you. Got that, okay?" She shooed us into an immaculate office and sat us both down by a computer, all while chatting away on the phone. She placed a stack of papers in our hands, and pointed at the top of the first one: *Sudan Media Contacts*.

Then she pointed at a document opened on her computer. It was her news story. Addy and I leaned in and began to read:

> *Government forces relocations from camps around Khartoum, which house around two million people mostly from Darfur and South Sudan, despite promises from the government they would be consulted before anyone was moved from the slum areas.*

Farah had included a quote from Jan Pronk, the UN Special Representative: "I deplore that strongly.... Promises have been made of consultation and I'm afraid to have to conclude that that consultation did not take place."

I had met Jan a few times, but could I really call him up and ask him for a quote? I gulped and glanced at Addy. Ready or not, things were about to get real and serious.

"Sorry about that ladies, I've got a million calls coming in. Addy, I've highlighted key contacts that work closely with Voices of America. Shannon, call Kristen. She's the UN Advocacy Adviser and she'll be your go-to person for most of your stories." Her phone rang and she stepped back out.

I called Kristen. "So you're Shannon, the new IRIN stringer? We're happy to have you on board!" She briefly informed me that the story according to the IDPs was that police surrounded them at 5:00 a.m. with guns and riot gear and then beat them without warning. The story according to the police and government was that security had been surrounded by IDPs armed with traditional weapons such as knives and axes, and nobody was shot or injured.

"The UN does not seek to dispute the facts on the ground," Kristen said on-record. "The issue that needs to be addressed is one of forced relocation. We support the government's intention to identify current locations of displacement in Khartoum; however, the process by which demolitions and relocations are being undertaken constitutes human rights violations, including forced return...."

The UN Office for the Coordination of Humanitarian Affairs (UN OCHA) in Khartoum stated that as of March 2005, the total number of IDPs in official camps and squatter areas in Khartoum was 2,072,320.

I spent four hours writing a 700-word news story for IRIN. It took that long because I wanted every sentence to be perfect. It was unlike writing for the *KM,* where proper English was undervalued; I was in the big leagues now. Erich, a die-hard perfectionist, ended up tossing most of my back story and adding his own. But on a positive note, he did keep a quote or two.

In time I got better at it. I had to. Erich was relentless about telling a compelling story in the best way possible. It was challenging to write and re-write one little news story. But it was

Erich's strict writing standards and learning to write in a crisis zone that helped me evolve into the writer I am today. This training would mean a lot for a girl who was beginning to dream about becoming a published author one day. Maybe I'd even write a book about my search for inner peace and sobriety in war-torn Sudan.

So bring on the challenges, I say.

\*\*\*

A few weeks later I was cruising in a cab to the UN OCHA building in Nairobi for the first day of IRIN's media training. There are more than twenty UN agencies operating in Kenya, including the worldwide headquarters of the UN Environment Program and UN-Habitat. Kenya hosts the largest refugee population in the world and faces a wide range of humanitarian crises, including drought, malnutrition and food insecurity, disease outbreaks, and internal conflicts over resources often compounded by political issues. Collectively, the UN in Kenya works to support the government in creating and sustaining an empowering environment for the promotion of human rights, good governance, and the improvement of the people's well-being by reducing poverty.

It wasn't even noon and already it had been one hell of a day. The plane was delayed for two hours in Cairo (which, okay, was kind of cool) but as soon as it landed in Nairobi, it began raining cats and dogs. Or how about warthogs and mongoose? In Kenya, it is desert warthogs and banded mongoose that run amok.

It was raining warthogs and mongoose, and the cab was about to get a flat tire.

"Seriously?" I huffed, peering out of the window as the driver fiddled in the back for a spare. I was an hour late. What would Erich think of me now? I wanted to put my best foot forward, but Kenya had other plans for me.

Once the cab driver fixed it, we were off—slowly. The roads were muddy. I proceeded to take pictures with my expensive, new camera through my window, which I had rolled down to let in the beautiful cool-hot Kenyan rain. Suddenly a random dude popped his hand through and grabbed for my camera.

"Hey!" I yelled and swatted his hand.

"Hey!" he yelled back. He was young, maybe fifteen. We tugged on the camera for a minute and then, like a kid sister fighting with her little brother, I pinched him. He squealed and scurried away.

Nairobi is known for its high crime rate. There are regular attacks on tourists by groups of armed assailants. Carjacking and "snatch and run" crimes are common, but the victims are not typically injured—as long as they don't resist.

We arrived at UN OCHA with two armed guards standing tall and firm at the front gate. They eyed me up and down suspiciously and refused to believe I was "Shannon from Sudan."

"Listen..." I started to tell them, but I got distracted as my cab driver grew impatient and drove off without me. So I stood in the rain defending my identity until a blond-haired woman in a silk shirt and pressed skirt rescued me.

"You must be our lost Sudanese?" she said and put her arm around my waist to steer me inside.

"Lost Sudanese?"

"Erich never clarified and there aren't many American freelance journalists hanging around Khartoum, so we just assumed..."

She rushed me down a corridor and into a brightly lit room where twenty journalists sat looking up at a projector. They were all African.

"Ah, Shannon. So good of you to join us," a husky male voice boomed at me. It was a short man with dark skin and a mysterious twinkle in his eye. Erich. There was something about his aura I liked right away.

"Everyone, this is Shannon of Sudan," he said. Erich motioned for me to take a seat and before I sat down he jumped right back into the training. I would learn quickly that this was how he rolled: structured, to the point, blunt, no fuss or muss.

I'd already made up my mind that I was going to be the perfect student, but this plan was quickly squashed. I could hardly see the images on the projector in front of me without contacts or glasses. Hermione of Harry Potter—the character I would model myself after during this training—would've made sure to bring some lenses; no doubt about it. This was so not my day.

"Never cut off part of a person's head when taking pictures." Erich flashed through images on the projector. "Otherwise, it will not be published. Think of interesting angles like this one." He pointed at the image with a red laser pointer. "Here WFP is doing a food drop in South Sudan and our stringer got underneath the plane as the delivery fell from the sky. If you choose to do something like this, please be smart about it and move out of the way before it's too late."

I wrote vigorously. *Never cut off a person's head. Be smart. Move out of the way before it's too late.*

The training continued until dinnertime. During the last few hours we discussed a more important aspect of writing for IRIN: the feature story. IRIN's features were longer articles (typically 900 to 1,500 words) and began by highlighting an individual affected by a humanitarian crisis. The middle portion of the article would highlight how the crisis affected a larger population and the article would end with an analysis of who, what, when, where, and why.

The feature resonated with me much more than a hot news story because it meant going in the field and interacting with people (as opposed to doing interviews over the phone) in order to understand all the facts, so one could offer realistic and effective solutions. I began to daydream about all the intriguing situations I'd heard about while living in Sudan: camel jockeys in Qatar, the issue of female genital mutilation, the tea ladies of Sudan, obstetric fistula, child prostitution. I couldn't wait to dig deep into each one.

"We are less of a hot news agency like Reuters or BBC and more of an informational tool used by various high-end parties, both political and humanitarian-based, especially in times of crisis. Our readers are dependent on IRIN not for the hot story but the *true* story," Erich's voice broke through my daydream.

"IRIN would rather verify that all facts presented are accurate even at the cost of being the last agency to post on the topic. So before you turn in a story, always be certain of where you are getting your facts and then verify with any applicable sources."

It was a lovely thing to say, but it wasn't necessarily accurate. As a stringer working for IRIN, which was funded by the UN, I discovered that certain facts of a story wouldn't be included if they could jeopardize strategic relationships the UN had with key political players. In defense of the UN, I understand that good working relationships have to be established even with Africa's Most Wanted; it is the only way to ensure entrance into a country to be able to help out those suffering from a crisis. In 2015, my experience was somewhat validated when IRIN released this statement on its website:

*After 19 years of award-winning coverage with the UN, we have started a new chapter. IRIN is now an independent, non-profit media organization. Outside of the UN, IRIN is in a better position to critically examine the multi-billion dollar humanitarian aid industry.*

After the training we all went to dinner at The Carnivore, an open-air restaurant that served a famous all-you-can-eat meat buffet. I kept thinking about PETA and my lifelong goal to be a vegetarian in order to honor my beloved animal friends, but as always—in the face of temptation—I fell short and scarfed down a plate of ostrich meatballs. It was the best meat I've ever tasted and still crave it to this day.

With a mouthful of crocodile, Erich, who sat next to me, leaned over. "Darfur is where it's at right now. Do you think you can get there?"

I was fairly green at all of this and getting to Darfur seemed like an impossible feat. "I can certainly try."

"IRIN's your ticket. Connect with the UN organizations on the ground in Khartoum. They have translators, vehicles, even planes on hand to help you in any way you need. Do what you can to get there, okay?"

My gut flipped. Translators, cars, and planes…oh my! Since landing in Khartoum, I'd felt the crisis in Darfur calling to me. It was like a really bad car accident, and I needed to see the wreckage with my own eyes. Perhaps so I could grasp how truly ugly humanity could be, and perhaps to wake up to my own fragility. With IRIN and Erich on my side, it was bound to happen.

\*\*\*

The next afternoon, IRIN loaded us into four vehicles that looked like monster trucks. I sat on the back seat sandwiched between Daniel of Uganda and Richard of Ethiopia. We had known each other only a few days, but already we were tight. The three of us were the only stringers that woke up early enough that morning to go on the safari IRIN had planned. It had been worth waking up for because we got to look for the "big five": the lion, elephant, buffalo, leopard, and rhinoceros. We also got stuck in the mud for a few hours right next to a lion's den, and since we'd thought we were going to be eaten for lunch, we were now bonded for life.

That afternoon we were headed to Kibera, the largest slum in Africa, and with over one million people it was one of the largest in the world. Most of Kibera's residents live in extreme poverty, earning less than one dollar per day. There is neither running water nor government clinics nor healthcare facilities. Malaria and tuberculosis are widespread and intensified by the cramped living conditions. Most health services are provided by churches and charitable organizations and the one we'd be working with was Medicines Sans Frontier (MSF), an international aid organization that provided medical care.

The assignment for the day was highlighting the issue of HIV and AIDs, which was highly prevalent in Kibera as a result of transactional sex. Prostitution was often a young girl's only means of survival, and young women traded their bodies for as little as twenty shillings ($0.30), just enough for a small meal. They were rarely in a position to negotiate the use of a condom. MSF ran an HIV clinic in Kibera's Gatwekera zone, which provided free diagnostic counseling and testing, psychosocial counseling, and antiretroviral therapy. IRIN wanted us to practice our interviewing and photography skills by interacting with the locals and the MSF staff.

Our trucks pulled up on a hill overlooking the slum. Right away I understood why Erich had asked our driver to pull over so I could stop at a local shop and trade my flip-flops for sneakers. Kibera consisted of tightly packed shacks with rusty grooved iron roofs. Each shack was roughly twelve by twelve feet in size, built with mud walls, concrete, and a dirt or concrete floor. The shacks often housed eight people or more, and many slept on the floor. Swirling around the shacks were streams of rotting sewage and garbage. One latrine was shared by up to fifty shacks, and the contents of the latrines sometimes overflowed into the walkways before being emptied out in a nearby river. I tried hard not to gag. Kibera smelled ten times worse than Khartoum on a bad day.

We made our way down the hill and my feet sunk several inches into a gooey walkway. I wondered what germs were festering in this gunk and what would've happened if Erich hadn't insisted we stop so I could change shoes. Could HIV cells seep into my shoes and penetrate my skin?

I thought of all the diseases that were running rampant in this place and was seized by panic. I'd never actually been face-to-face with a person with HIV or AIDS (at least that I knew of). Did I have any open wounds? What if I had a minor cut and one of the residents grazed my skin in that exact spot? I was uneducated about how it all worked and terrified at the thought of discussing it with someone. What would I say? I squirmed in my skin, trying to keep it together while silently praying for the panic attacks to stay at bay.

*It's okay, Shan. Just keep your cool and try not to touch anyone.*

Through a narrow walkway and up a short incline we were greeted by a group of African men and women and a handful of MSF staff. Everyone stood in brightly colored t-shirts. On the front of the shirts were the words *HIV Positive*. On the back: *I know. Do you?*

A woman greeted us in a Kenyan accent with blindingly white teeth. She was young, maybe thirty, and had a stunning smile that would melt the heart of any man. She greeted everyone individually with a handshake, and when she did, she looked intensely in their eyes and said, "Welcome to Kibera."

As she moved toward me, my throat stiffened. I didn't want to touch her. Was it necessary in order for me to capture the story? I didn't think so, but I couldn't necessarily pull away either.

"Welcome." She was in front of me now. She held out her hand and I shook it begrudgingly. Her skin was warm, coarse. When she was done greeting everyone, she motioned for our group to sit on chairs that had been placed in three short rows on a grassy null.

"My name is Samia and I heard about MSF at the end of 2002, during MSF's campaign for World AIDS Day in Kenya. I thought I might have HIV or AIDS, but I was ashamed and so I called MSF and made up a story that it was my sister who was infected with the virus. I wanted more information. The following month, I began to get treatment and participate in MSF's support groups for the first time.

"For years I denied the fact that I was infected with HIV. I told myself that the testing machines did not work properly. But the support groups helped me to finally accept the truth, and I began to be okay with it. Now I talk openly about this disease and offer support to as many people as possible. I can be compassionate and empathetic with these people because I know what they're going through. It's my life experience, not something I know from a book."

Encouraged by the MSF team, Samia created a support group herself and its members meet up every two weeks to share what they are going through, discuss AIDS prevention, and help people in denial accept their situations. After Samia's introduction we were encouraged to ask questions.

Keeping Hermione in mind, I raised my hand. "How does your community treat you when you wear a shirt like that?" I asked.

"Since I found out that I have the virus, I lost all my old friends. But I have made others who have HIV/AIDS also and help me reach my goals. Together we work hard to convince our community leaders to accept the reality of HIV/AIDS. We tell them, 'We are young, sexually active. Are we going to infect people?' We all concluded that promoting condoms is necessary." (The majority of people in Kibera were Muslim and sex before marriage was a taboo.)

Then Heather, an MSF Project Coordinator, stood up. "I'm proud of these women here today, for they are living strong despite the ridicule they receive on a daily basis." Heather wasn't HIV positive, but she sported a t-shirt like the others. "We try to let these people know that despite the disease, they can live happy and healthy lives with treatment and support. They can go on to having a purpose and give back to their community. It doesn't have to be a death sentence; it can be a 'reason for living' sentence, and that's how they're learning to view it."

After we had the chance to conduct one-on-one interviews, Samia walked over with a handful of her friends in t-shirts. "We want to thank you for coming to our home and for sharing our stories with the world," she said.

I was still concerned about touching these HIV-infected people, but in spite of this, I extended my arms and gave Samia and her friends a hug. It was an important gesture for me to do consciously because I wanted to work on the irrational fears I'd associated with this disease and eliminate them.

This experience is more significant to me today than it was then. As a person who struggled for nearly fifteen years with drug and alcohol addiction, I know what it's like to be stigmatized and ashamed. In 2011, after my third DUI landed me in jail, I was convicted of a felony DUI. The innocent person I thought I was, sweet Shan, was now a criminal. The experience was terrifying enough to sober me up, but my felony and the stigma that came with it were still hard for me to accept, so I didn't; I hid from most of the people who knew me and pretended that my addiction wasn't that bad.

The more I hid it, the more powerful was my shame.

After two years in recovery, I realized that even though I was *sober* and had come very far in my recovery process, I was stuck emotionally, spiritually, and mentally. One night before bed I realized why: I was hiding a huge part of *my life journey*, and through this one seemingly small act, I was, in a sense, isolating, rejecting, and judging *myself*.

That night I decided to take a risk and spill my guts in a 700-word status update on Facebook. In my update I shared my addiction story, including many of the things I was most ashamed of. My ugly past was finally out there for everyone to like or dislike and even comment on. It was terrifying, but at the same time I felt so incredibly free. My status update went something like this:

*My name is Shannon Mae Egan and I've struggled with an addiction to drugs and alcohol for nearly fifteen years of my life. I am a convicted felon with three DUIs. I've spent time in jail, and I was on house arrest for sixty days and court-ordered probation for several years. Up until this point, I've kept this a secret because I was ashamed. I didn't know how YOU, my friends and family around the world, would receive me…*

The next day I woke up to find that the post had been shared around the world, and in less than eight hours, it had garnered over 400 likes, 140 comments, and spurred a ton of messages in my inbox from people I knew and didn't know. Their feedback pretty much all said the same thing:

*Thank you for sharing your story. You've given me hope that recovery is possible.*

I couldn't believe it. Many of the people I thought would judge me were accepting and supportive. They had family members and friends struggling with addiction, too, and some were trying to find recovery themselves.

Just like Samia's phone call to MSF, one bold act transformed my life more than any other because for the first time I was making a public statement that said: *I accept and love all of myself just as I am—even the ugly, disgraceful parts.*

Love and acceptance. This is what healed my shame.

# Chapter 8

oseph stood on a makeshift stage in front of the entire BES student body looking like his spirit had been sucked from his body by a covert Martian space invader. This was concerning because he was supposed to be leading the other boys in a smooth dance routine to the beat of "Yeah!" by Usher, Lil Jon, and Ludacris.

As Joseph stood motionless and withdrawn, Usher bellowed out the words: *Up in the club with my homies, tryna get a li'l V-I, but keep it down on the low key...*

I stood on the side of the stage to give the boys cues. Via ESP, I sent Joseph a message: *You've got this! Smile!*

It seemed to work—sort of? He began to dance, but instead of doing the step sequence we'd been practicing for the last four weeks, he busted out his own moves on the fly. I couldn't tell if he was doing the running man, the robot, or simply jogging in place.

*No, no, no! What's that? That's not our choreography!*

From the stage, Mohammed, Ebrahim, and Yusif looked over at me in bafflement as butterflies mimicked Joseph's moves in my stomach. I waved my arms in a passionate circle, which meant that they were to ignore Joseph and begin the routine. They got the jest of what I was trying to say and started in. They were all decked out in tiny black suits with colorful ties, and even with Joseph doing whatever it was he was doing, they were four of the most sophisticated third-graders I'd seen in my life. I beamed.

The girls were up next. They had on dazzling glittery dresses with pink and red hues splashed across their lips and bows in their braided hair. Running past me to the stage, they held out their hands for me to high five them. I suddenly remembered to breathe before I passed out.

"Teacher, you need to chill out! It's just a dance!" Dalila shouted as she gave me a high five.

This was funny because that morning, during our last rehearsal, I'd told them the exact same thing. Along with: "Remember, its one moment in time and when it's all over you're going to wish it wasn't, so give it all you've got!"

But I was a bundle of nerves. In my defense, I knew how hard they'd practiced for this moment and how nervous they were about it. I worried that if they messed up they'd internalize the experience and be afraid to try new things forever. I wanted to protect them from this. I wanted to protect them from everything.

The girls performed flawlessly. When they were done, we found our designated row and sat down, all nine of us. It was the last day of school and the last time we would sit in this capacity, as a team. We'd accomplished so much together in the last year. I could hardly believe I was the person who introduced them to times tables and taught them about snowboarding. Would they ever really know how much they meant to me? I'd been choked up all night thinking about our final goodbye.

"Did you see that, man? Everybody loved it! They were dancing in their seats," Joseph said from his chair beside Yusif.

"Teacher, you were so nervous. You were shaking!" Rashida said, resting her head on my arm. I slid down in my seat so she could more comfortably rest on my shoulder.

"No way, I knew you could do it. You guys were awesome."

Ebrahim plopped his petite body in my lap. "Teacher! Who you kiddin'? You were so scared! More scared than us!"

"Guys, I was only acting nervous because I wanted to see how well you'd do under pressure, *hello!*"

"Whatever, teacher. We know your tricks," he said. That was the line I teased *them* with all the time. My eyes watered.

"Oh yeah?" I asked. Ebrahim looked at me and with one finger he dabbed at a tear lingering in the corner of my eye.

"Man, the dust is crazy today. My eyes are killing me." I rubbed at them.

Ebrahim gave me a long look, and instead of sassing back like I expected him too, he snuggled into me. Saara rested her head on my other shoulder and placed her hand in mine. The next class got up to perform and I was glad that the music was loud so that I could clear my throat and hide my sniffles without the kids noticing. They were one of the best things that ever happened to me. I would miss them terribly from this day forward. Even ten years later, whenever I thought of them, my heart would light up with pure, untainted joy.

But the show had to go on.

\*\*\*

I spent a big portion of my end-of-school stipend on a plane ticket to Greece. I told myself that I deserved a non-work related adventure now that school was over, and after a year of nearly losing my hair and having to sleep on a hard, tweed bed, learning to successfully navigate the world of local and international news, and after my friendship with Addy had unexpectedly crumbled. It was time for a little play, especially considering I was all signed up for a *second year in Sudan*.

For year two, I'd be teaching third graders at Unity High School, an independent, British-style school, which was bigger and better than BES in every way. It provided an education to children four to eighteen years of age with a total of 750 students. I would teach roughly twenty-five students in an enormous classroom complete with all the teaching supplies I could ever dream of *and* I would receive a huge increase in my salary and move into an elegant apartment right next door to the school, which came with a satellite TV and garbage disposal. In my room I had a king-sized bed with a real mattress and my own balcony.

I was beyond stoked for the future. The Sudanese seemed enthusiastic as well. They'd gotten into a rhythm with the peace process, and if they couldn't find a way to work out the kinks they were figuring out how to work around them—at least temporarily. The most positive thing to date was that John Garang had been sworn in as the first vice-president. During his inauguration ceremony, he and President Omar al-Bashir had signed a power-sharing constitution and sealed it with a handshake. It was an emotional experience for everyone because nobody, including me, had known for sure that Sudan would make it that far.

I was all set for Greece—or so I thought. According to the Ministry of Humanitarian Affairs, I owed several thousands of dollars in taxes, and the tax officers weren't going to let me leave the country unless I paid up. I had assumed BES was paying for them out of my salary like my previous employer had done for me in America, so I contacted Fifi about it and she assured me this was the case. However, *somebody* was lying because the tax people never got the money.

I didn't know what to do, but needed to figure it out quickly because I was supposed to be in Athens in just two days. Luckily, my buck-toothed and eccentric friend, Amir—a well-known and successful artist—knew everybody. He knew how to work the system too. Around town people loved him for this, but they also thought he was clinically insane. He genuinely believed he was an African Prince and that my name was Chanel (even though I'd told him otherwise a million times). At the Ministry of Humanitarian Affairs, Amir used his swagger to address the tax representatives on my behalf. After a five-minute spiel it was obvious they weren't budging. This infuriated Amir and he began screaming ferociously in Arabic while waving his arms above his head and hopping from one foot to the other. I was mortified. Yet moments later there was some discussion among the workers, I received a few sideways glances, and then they handed Amir a piece of paper. That was it. We were done.

"What did you say to them?" I asked as we were exiting the building.

"I told them you had a life-threatening disease and you needed a shot from your American doctor in the next 48 hours or you would die."

*Why didn't I think of that?* I wondered.

"I also told them you were famous in America and good friends with Bush. This is why they didn't want your blood on their hands."

Thanks to Amir I got to see the Acropolis and the Temple of Olympian Zeus, but my favorite part of Greece was the clean showers and innumerable pastry shops; they were everywhere and filled with fluffy, flaky, sugary goods that melted on the tongue. I've always been a sucker for a pastry.

Toward the end of my vacation, I decided to camp out at an internet café in the heart of Athens (surrounded by a dozen pastry shops) so I could type in my digital journal. With my laptop in front of me and the most delectable chocolate croissant— my third one that day—in hand, I cozied in, ready to write and reflect.

*Saturday, July 30th, 2005*

*ATHENS! This is a dream come true. I'm sober, too. It's been a while now since my last relapse and things are starting to fall into place. I found something that I'm good at and that fulfills me creatively. The sky's the limit! Plus, I didn't have one drink on this trip despite the fact that there are bars everywhere—be proud, Shan! You've got this!!*

I typed deep in thought until I was interrupted by a ding. It was Instant Messenger alerting me that I had a memo. I picked up the croissant and took a bite before switching over to my Yahoo account. The message was from Erich. It read:

*Where's the Garang story?*

I swallowed a mouthful of gooey croissant. *Garang story?* I typed back.

*Seriously, Shannon? WHERE THE HELL ARE YOU?*

Blood rushed my face and neck. I stared at the screen. Something was wrong, *terribly wrong*. I waited for Erich to type back and explain, but he never did. Anxiety pulsed through my veins like a diesel-powered high-speed train. Dr. John Garang was the cornerstone of the peace agreement. If anything happened to him...

I hesitated before logging onto the Sudan news feed. I didn't want anything to ruin my perfect vacation or my perfect croissant. After all, I was in Greece for the very first time and I deserved this. Right? A few seconds passed. It was no use. I was worried for my Sudanese friends, and as a journalist, I was curious about the potential drama unfolding back in Khartoum. I'd face time and again throughout my journalism career the tension between those two feelings, but at this point, I had little experience to go off of.

I took another bite and began to spell out Garang's name in a search engine. Before I finished typing, two words auto-populated that made my heart stop:

*Garang death.*

I clicked on it.

Below were dozens of links explaining the situation in more detail. The first one read:

*Garang Killed in Plane Crash, Riots Erupt in Khartoum*

My mouth dropped open. I immediately understood the reason for the rioting: *the southerners suspect foul play.* I knew this because this was my first thought and I wasn't a conspiracy theorist by any stretch of the imagination.

Dead? In a plane crash? A few weeks after his inauguration? *How convenient.*

In my dismay I'd smooshed the croissant between my fingers. Chocolate guts oozed everywhere. I wiped my hand with a napkin, eyes still glued to the screen. I found an article written for *The Guardian* that confirmed my suspicions:

*Riot police were deployed to several areas of Khartoum where crowds were pelting passers-by with stones and smashing car windows. Khartoum's governor imposed a curfew on the capital from 6 p.m. to 6 a.m. Police officers told Reuters there were 24 victims of the violence in the city hospital's morgue.*

*"Murderers! Murderers!" yelled some southern Sudanese protesters who alleged the Sudanese government, which had battled Mr. Garang's rebel force for two decades before this year's peace deals, may have been behind the crash.*

Other outlets reported that Garang's plane crashed into a mountain range in southern Sudan upon returning home from a meeting with the President of Uganda, a close ally of Garang's. Fourteen people had gone down with him despite the fact that hours earlier an official announcement had been made indicating Garang's plane had landed safely. The culprit for the crash: bad weather and bad visibility. Yet the black box was either destroyed or missing. Weren't they supposed to be indestructible? I could hardly believe what I was reading. Before I could finish I was interrupted by another ding on my computer. It was Addy. She'd signed up for another year, too, and would be teaching at Unity alongside me while working for Voices of America.

*Our neighborhood is under siege! There are guns, bombs. Barricaded self into building with old man. Not allowed to move. Got sound footage of explosions. At Hotel Meridian hiding. Are you okay?*

Adrenaline shot through my body like a lightning bolt.

*OMG! Yes, in Greece on vacay! Are you OK?* I typed back.

It was nice of Addy to check in, but honestly? I was jealous. I knew a story like this could mean everything for a journalist's career. Breaking news topics (such as war, earthquakes, or other natural disasters) were much easier to sell to editors, as opposed to the coverage of chronic issues (poverty, disease, and famine). I know how terrible this sounds and writing it even now makes me cringe, but the higher the death toll, the more gripping the visual, and therefore the more compelling the story. This meant more readers and increased credibility with editors, which made us look like a bunch of bloodthirsty, nymphomaniac parasites getting off on the death and destruction of innocent lives and communities. But let it be noted that the international media machine (which includes news agencies, editors, journalists, politicians, the UN, and press representatives working for the humanitarian aid industry) was a mega-watt complicated cluster and everyone had a hand in it...even *readers*.

Typically, journalists are passionate about sharing stories with the world in order to bring in donors. But if blood and guts is what the public is interested in reading, who are we to argue? Often times, a terrifying visual is the only way to generate interest and therefore establish funding for critical humanitarian aid, which creates an intense practical and ethical dilemma for journalists world-wide. But again, at that particular moment in time, these issues were neither here nor there. Later, I'd become acutely aware of them, but only after hours of field work and later in Darfur when all hell broke loose.

Without even flinching over the possible dangers, I turned a razor-sharp focus toward flying back to Khartoum. I logged into the Sudan news feed and discovered a spine-chilling warning from the U.S. Embassy in Khartoum: *American citizens are urged to avoid all non-essential travel to Sudan at this time and those within Sudan are advised to stay indoors in a safe area due to disturbances in Khartoum and the suburbs.* Disregarding this, I emailed Alfie, the headmaster at Unity, for help arranging a driver from the airport. I typed rapidly. I heard another ding — Addy again:

*Shopkeepers sweeping up glass, smoke and light flashes from presidential palace, armed soldiers and police stopping cars, pedestrians. I saw a man in the street being beaten and there were bombs just up the street, gunshots all over.*

Alfie was online too and sent a response to my email: *I shall be coming to pick you up at the airport. No problem.*

And then not even two minutes later he wrote: *Ignore my last email! The airport is closed right now and the advice from everyone is do not get on a flight to Khartoum — they probably won't fly anyway!*

I wrote Addy, Alfie, and Erich the same message:

*I'm getting on a plane and I'm coming to Khartoum.*

Alfie wished me luck, Erich didn't respond, and Addy cautioned: *Get ready for a storm.*

\*\*\*

The streets of Khartoum were empty except for a creepy atmosphere that lingered thickly, stagnant in the air as if a highly toxic *haboob* had blown through and wiped out everyone in its path. There wasn't a rickshaw, tea lady, starving animal, or legless beggar in sight. I'd never seen the city *so quiet* and it was very unnerving. After three days of unrest, the death toll was up to one hundred and there had been reports of gangs prowling the streets with clubs, knives, and guns in total disregard for the curfew, so it made sense why everyone was hiding.

Although it was mid-day and there wasn't a gang member in sight, my driver was furious to be on the road.

"Don't you know? We are in the middle of a war!" he hissed.

In the rearview mirror of the cab, I watched his eyes dart feverishly from side to side as he ducked low in his seat. During the drive from the airport I saw the damage with my own eyes: dozens of buildings had been caught in the crossfire. Their walls were smothered in soot and the windows had giant shards of glass sticking out. Curbside, a handful of cars had been reduced to metal frames by fire.

I didn't respond to the driver because I *did* know that Sudan was in the middle of a war and yet I had chosen to come. Now that I was here, I realized that the idea of a war-zone had been a cliché in my mind. An *adventure*. I'd already been through a coup and survived—no problem. But this situation felt different. During the coup I'd never seen bombings or bloodshed; for the most part, life had gone on as usual. Why had I rushed into coming back here? People were dying—actually dying—to get out and I'd pulled tooth and nails to get in. Was I mad? What if I'd been here and witnessed the bombings and violent attacks with my own eyes? How would I feel then? In the car that day I didn't feel much of anything. I hadn't slept in over forty-eight hours and my body had been running on adrenaline ever since I'd heard of Garang's death. I lacked the capacity, dangerously, to reflect.

The cab turned down the road to my new apartment and I saw that the building across the street was also smudged in black. Its windows were jagged or missing completely. Goosebumps pricked my arms. This was so close to home. Too close. The driver pulled in front of my complex, which was protected by a towering metal gate. He stopped the car and I hesitated for a minute before getting out.

"Why do you sit? Go!" he snarled, startling me. He was waiting for me to change my clothes so he could take me to my next destination: a press conference where Jan Pronk was set to address the media about any new discoveries connected to Garang's death. I needed to be there in an hour.

I jumped out of the car, grabbed my bags, and pounded on the gate. I still didn't have a gate key because Alfie was working on changing the locks, but he promised that our gatekeeper would be there to let me in. I pounded again as goosebumps spread over to my neck. I felt like Bambi's mom in Disney's cartoon film. She'd been shot dead while enjoying fresh spring grass in a wide-open field. I was innocent and exposed; the rioters were armed and dangerous.

*Were they hunting me now?* I wondered. Spooking myself, I spun to the left and squinted at the shattered windows for a better look.

Then, from inside the complex, I heard feet slapping on the pavement.

"*Is makminoo?*" a voiced demanded in Arabic.

"*Isme* Shannon!" I swore.

With an earsplitting screech the gate opened. A face peered out from behind it: Luke, our gatekeeper. We'd met a few times already. He grabbed the suitcase from my hand and shoved me with it from behind to try and hurry me along. It hit the back of my leg and my knees bent. I stumbled, nearly falling over. He apologized, but said that he and our complex had been a target during the riots because he'd let a journalist up on the roof to take pictures. Luke wanted us both inside where we were safe.

"This journalist!" Luke shook his head disapprovingly. "He take pictures. Put us all in danger. *Mushkilla kabeera!*"

While Luke was infuriated over this man's actions, I found them absurdly comforting. I wasn't the only person caught up in the drama unfolding around us. During my correspondence with Addy over the last couple of days, I'd found her to be positively electrified by it. I thought of the IM she'd written while I was in Greece:

*Got sounds of the blasts for news footage!*

Clearly we had a lot to learn about what it meant to be writers for real people living in real-life emergency situations. Addy was a highly intelligent, strong-willed, and insecure girl. Like me, she suffered from terribly low self-esteem, and having our stories published for big-name agencies helped us fill voids that, as young people, we didn't know how else to fill.

I rushed into my apartment, threw on a fresh change of clothes, and brushed my teeth. I was back in the cab less than five minutes later. On our way to the press conference, I asked the driver to swing by *Shar'ea* Mohammed Nageed. I wanted to check the status of my old stomping grounds. Erich had asked for pictures of the wreckage, so I whipped out my camera and began shooting mindlessly at the blackened cars on the side of the street. Across from BES, I saw that Ozone, the restaurant I'd eaten at during BES lunch breaks, had been hit. Other nearby businesses had been engulfed in flames and all that remained were metal skeletons and ash. I got my video camera out so I could document the situation and leaned out the window for a close-up.

Off in the distance, I heard screaming. I looked behind us to see a group of agitated police officers in blue jumpsuits and black berets running toward us.

"*Khawaja! Khawaja!*" the officers screamed. They shouted for us to stop the car, machine guns waving.

"*Oh no...*" I whispered, dropping the camcorder in my lap.

My heart burned as if a wildfire had ignited inside it. I'd heard that taking photos and video footage was *haram* in Islam and against Sharia Law. If this were true, the police officers could legally confiscate my equipment, jail me, or worse.

*Was public flogging part of the punishment for breaking this rule?* I wondered.

The driver stopped the car and within seconds the officers were at our side. They yanked open the doors, pulled us out, and chucked us to the ground like we were a couple of useless cargo crates. As my body hit the earth, clouds of dust puffed up and into my lungs. I coughed. The police officers grabbed us by our arms and dragged us to a nearby tree where we were forced to sit on two metal chairs. Petrified, I stared at the ground. By now, the wildfire was passionately ablaze throughout my entire body. My arm stung where the officer's hand had been. Beside me, my driver quivered. I felt terrible for getting him into this mess, but it was too late to apologize now. We were in serious trouble.

"*El-Jawaz!*" the officers commanded. *Passport!* I didn't have it on me. This infuriated them.

One of the officers lifted my chin with the tip of his Kalashnikov. The metal was warm. I winced, too exhausted and panicked to do much else. In a rage, he began yelling at me as he held up my video camera and pulled out a tape. I tried to swallow.

"*Min wen?*" Their tone was hostile.

"*Ana min Amerika,*" I said, rolling the 'r' like the Sudanese. The officers glared at me. "*Amerika? Walahi?*" *Really?*

"*Naam,*" I coughed wearily. "*Ana ustaza. Englezeya.*" I stumbled over my Arabic. *I'm an English teacher.*

"*Baa'ref Arabee shwaya,*" I continued. *I only speak a little Arabic.*

He asked me if I was a journalist and I swore that I wasn't. If he searched my bag, he'd find my press pass and I'd be screwed *big time*. The one in charge eyed me up and down. He motioned for the others to search my bag. Behind me, I heard the clasp of my media pack open. I coughed again.

"*Min fadlak, ana marsha madrassa,*" I begged coarsely. *If you please, I'm headed to the school.*

"*Askotti!*" *Be quiet!*

Down the road, a blast sounded and we all flinched. We turned in the direction of the noise but didn't see anything.

Another explosion went off. *Boom!*

"*Besora'a! Emshe!*" the officers yelled at us. *Hurry! Get out of here!*

One of the officers jerked me up by my shirt and pushed me toward the cab. Waving their guns, they continued to howl at us. I knew that the only reason we were getting off was because there was a bigger threat close by. I hopped into the front of the cab next to the driver with my equipment in hand and slammed the door.

Without skipping a beat, the cab driver turned on the car and we sped off. As dust clouds rushed after us, the driver began to berate me angrily. His voice was beyond thrill, and a giant vein—which I hadn't noticed before—bulged and throbbed on his forehead. Another blast reverberated in the distance. The driver stopped yelling and we both looked back. I heard the distinctive sound of glass shattering and metal scraping. Starting in on me again, the driver shrieked, but this time I cut him off.

"*Halas!*" I yelled fiercely and covered my ears. *Stop!*

Then I felt bad for losing my temper. "*Ana asif. Giddam. Giddam!*" I apologized, and encouraged him to keep going. My face was frantic and pale in the side mirror.

William had once said to me, "When Sudanese engage in war, they really go at it. They are brutal fighters. If a war were to ever start in Khartoum, there will be no saving you."

At the thought of him my face fell. Was he okay? Were my students okay? I looked toward the sky for a hint of a silver lining, but all I saw was dust.

\*\*\*

"They did it!" William yelled bitterly referring to the Sudanese government.

We were having tea at the *Khartoum Monitor* a few days later. The riots had settled a bit and the Sudanese were starting to come out of hiding and begin their daily routines. In the last twenty-four hours not one death had been reported, which we all considered a miracle.

"We have been fighting for peace for twenty-two years and now it's gone just like that!" William slammed his fist on the desk in front of him. His eyes were bloodshot and there were swollen, purple circles underneath. He looked as if he hadn't slept in weeks.

It was unsettling to see him this way. He was typically so cool and composed. He'd been my rock, offering up endless tidbits of wisdom and hope for the future of Sudan. But the man sitting before me was broken. I could only imagine how hard the news of Garang's death had been on him. William told me once that although he'd never met Garang in person he *knew* him in his heart, where it mattered most. William thought of him as his brother who'd been out in the bush fighting for the rights of his family all these years.

Most of the southern Sudanese felt that way.

Over the last few days, I had conducted interviews with both northerners and southerners whose businesses had been destroyed in the riots. The riots had exposed the deep-seated hatred they had for each other, but nobody indicated that they thought Garang's death was a good thing. The general consensus was that Garang had—in his own crooked way—brought the idea of peace and equality to Sudan, and these things were essential to everyone's well-being and the future of the country.

For the southerners, Garang's death was particularly hard. They mourned the loss of their champion like he was a family member.

In the aftermath, they could barely function. It was my first time conducting interviews with people who were in the middle of an emergency, and as I coaxed them into talking about the tragedy and their resulting suffering, I tried to be gentle about it. But I felt like a fraud as I sat with the Sudanese, *my friends*, and pried into their lives knowing I was there to exploit them. I was going to sell their pain to the public for financial gain. The more heartache they expressed, the better my story. It felt manipulative and invasive, and I didn't know what to do. I wanted to keep my cool new job, so I brushed off my discomfort and got the story to IRIN.

"Look me in the eyes, Shannon, and you tell me that you believe Garang's death was an accident!"

I thought back to the recent press conference with Jan Pronk who'd reiterated that the plane had simply crashed due to bad weather and lack of visibility. He'd said, "I have seen with my own eyes how the President was shaken [by the news of Garang's death]. The government is definitely not behind this."

Despite Pronk's reassurance, I couldn't believe him.

"Ah ha! See? You look away because you know the truth. This was a declaration of war! They get to keep everything the same and we get nothing. The CPA will be postponed; the south will have no autonomy, no referendum, no rights."

He slumped down into his chair and hung his head.

"William?" I said softly. "You know what Mr. Pronk said to the media the other day? He said if you loved Garang as a leader than you have to follow him to peace. Dr. Garang's wife, Rebecca? She urged everyone to remain calm and to remember that the only way to keep Garang's memory alive is to move his vision forward." I paused, my heart breaking for my friend.

"Sudan has come too far. *You've* come too far and you can't give up. Not now."

As if my words stung him, William flinched. "I just don't know how peace will ever find us. Not after this."

# Chapter 9

*I* sat in a chair next to William and placed a hand on his shoulder. "I understand. But what if the outcome depended entirely on how you viewed the situation? You can focus on Garang's death or you can focus on his mission and the peace deal that your paper has been pushing for so many years. You're the one that's always saying to me that there's a lesson and an opportunity in every situation."

Slouched over, William didn't respond. I fell silent and found myself getting lost in thought. The Sudanese reaction to Garang's death reminded me of something that I had a lot of experience in: *relapse*. Like a struggling alcoholic faced with a crisis, the Sudanese had fallen back on old behavior patterns because their new coping skills were fragile. And Garang's death wasn't just *any* crisis. It was a full-on catastrophe that threatened their basic human rights. Considering Sudan's brutally violent history, which goes back thousands of years—long before the second civil war—it was a shock that Garang's death didn't ignite a third. In Khartoum, where tensions were particularly high, the riots lasted less than seven days. This was a relatively quick turnaround.

To me, this was a testament of their strength of character and how truly dedicated they were to peace. I wished that William could see this.

I found it interesting that it was so easy for me to cheer the Sudanese on during their dark hour considering that my relapse pattern was to mentally and emotionally beat the crap out of myself—for my own good, of course! At least, this is how I sold it. Part of me thought that guilt was an effective tool for ensuring that I'd never drink again, which was pretty ludicrous considering it *never* worked—not long-term. It was a form of self-harm, and harm of any kind only creates more fear and more pain. In the end I always ran back to the bottle, frantic for reprieve from my own harsh punishments.

*Where had I learned this technique?* I wondered. Dr. Reynolds's gentle voice popped in my head:

*Later, as an adult parent, your mom abused you, her child— whom she loves and adores—because she believed that the punishments acted out on her were done out of love. This is what she was told. Your mom was probably unaware that the violence she endured was directly related to the fact that her parents were beaten also. And now here you are today, Shannon, carrying the pattern forward.*

The more I thought about this, the more insane it sounded. I was beating up on myself—*out of love*—in the hope that it would help me quit. It was one of those light bulb moments.

"William! I will come and visit you tomorrow. Okay?" I gave him a side hug just like Dr. Reynolds used to give to me and rushed home, eager to write. I had an important idea I wanted to jot down in my journal before I forgot all about it:

*Friday, August 5th, 2005*

*The next time you relapse—which I doubt you will because you're doing so awesome!—try being kind and loving to yourself like you were with the Sudanese today. And they killed people,*

*Shan. If you can find compassion for them, you should be able to give it to yourself too. Focus on the positive and how far you've come. It will make it easier for you to get back up. Don't you forget this. (I have a feeling you will.)*

Garang's death went down in the history books as an accident. Yet the circumstances surrounding it are still widely debated. Today there are countless online forums dedicated to uncovering the truth and they all pose the same question: who killed Dr. John Garang? Perhaps we'll never know.

In 2007, Garang's wife, Rebecca, who had remained mum on the matter, finally broke her silence in a ceremony in Nairobi where Garang was honored with a posthumous Uhuru Award for his contribution to the liberation of Sudan. She said:

"When my husband died, I did not come out openly and say he was killed because I knew the consequences. At the back of my mind, I knew my husband had been assassinated. I was one of many people who refused to accept the immediate conclusion then that it was an accident. Not because we missed Garang too much and found it impossible to let go, which we did, but because the explanation was too obvious. If anyone wanted to kill Garang (and there were many forces) there was no better cover for an almost perfect crime than for him to be traveling unofficially in the helicopter of his closest ally."

In this same statement, Rebecca said that her first suspect was and still remains the Sudanese government, and that a "black prophet arising from the south must seem like the end of the world for them. They feared that Garang had the potential of turning the country into a genuinely democratic environment where Sudanese might, in the Martin Luther King hope, 'be judged not by the color of their skin but by the content of their character.'"

In the same year that Rebecca spoke out, I was living the good life in New York City and writing for the UN Population

Fund. I'd landed a writing contract to publish *this* story with a literary agent, the late Carolyn French, who worked for Fifi Oscard, a renowned agency that lists William Shatner as a client. In the eyes of our world, I was on top of it. But inside I was a mess and I relapsed, *hard*. In a nasty downward spiral — where I would eventually lose everything—I fell back into my old patterns of mental and emotional abuse, and those patterns carried on for years.

But today, after having invested copious amounts of time into obtaining inner peace, I know that kindness and compassion are far more effective tools than shame and guilt. In fact, they are *the* two most effective tools in helping me establish recovery long-term. Since relapse is so common among individuals who are struggling with drug and alcohol addiction (70 to 90 percent experience relapse) it makes more sense for our recovering community to embrace the idea that *setbacks will happen*. What if—given our history—we even viewed relapse as a natural and understandable part of the recovery process? What if we embraced it as an opportunity to learn, heal, and grow?

What if instead of kicking ourselves when we were down, we focused on the positive aspects of our journey and tried to remember just how far we've come?

\*\*\*

By mid-November life had resumed as usual. I'd written a handful of hot news stories and I had half a dozen features in the queue for IRIN. The United Nations Mission in Sudan had connected me with Bushra, a delicately framed but energetic Sudanese man who worked for the UN as a translator.

With a voice recorder in hand and a pen and notepad in the other, Bushra and I set out to investigate the various humanitarian crises affecting those living in Khartoum and its surrounding suburbs. So far we'd investigated the issue of children growing up in Omdurman's women's prison while their mothers served a twenty-year sentence for selling drugs and alcohol. We'd been to Ombara to interview young girls about prostitution, and their experiences were similar to those engaging in transactional sex in Kibera. After so many hours in the field, one thing was becoming distinctively clear: journalism was tough work.

More often than not I found myself doing something—deliberately or accidentally—that was in direct contradiction with the ethics and standards of journalism. In a nutshell, this ethical code, (which varies from country to country and organization to organization) provides a general set of principles meant to guide journalists through various work-related challenges. For instance, it's expected of journalists to report news accurately and fairly. It is also expected that one should avoid journalistic "scandals" at all costs. This includes fabrication and omission. As a stringer for IRIN, I was having to omit critical details *all the time*, especially if they pointed fingers at the Sudanese government or questioned UN motives and structure. Often I'd have to manipulate content so that the story fit into IRIN's particular agenda, which, to me, felt like fabrication.

To further complicate matters, it is considered unethical for a journalist to accept favors from organizations that he or she is writing about. The reason is obvious: gifts create biases. But the UN had offered up transportation and a translator, two essentials for a foreign freelancer writing in a war zone. It's nearly impossible for a stringer to write a story without the help of organizations on the ground. And those that do help have a vested interest; they need stringers to promote their issues and work. Without us, there are no stories, no public, no funding. (Okay, maybe it's not *that* extreme, but it would certainly limit their exposure and the donor pool.) Unable to compete with organizations with deep pockets, the agendas of smaller humanitarian aid originations often went unnoticed, creating an unfair advantage for real-life issues that the public should know about. The only real solution I could imagine was to develop an independent funding mechanism for journalists' expenses, so stories could be told truthfully and accurately, no strings attached.

In the meantime, I had to work with what *was* instead of what *should be*, and I accepted Bushra and his valuable skillset with open arms. He was lighthearted and enjoyed the work, which was crucial because the hours were long and the interviews taxing. Stories took considerable time to unravel, so we worked on many all at once. To get to the heart of an issue, one feature might require a dozen interviews with a variety of people, including professors, local authorities, and community members. I enjoyed the work. I was no longer pretending to investigate important issues that mattered to the world; I was doing it *for real*. My note-taking skills and adventurous daydreaming had come in handy after all.

But there was another barrier to being an effective, honest storyteller: *me*. Through my fieldwork, I was learning that I was unclear on a lot of really important things, such as my own intentions, motivations, and reactions. Without self-awareness I would add to these already complicated clusters instead of contributing to their solution, making me a real threat to society. As the spiritual speaker and writer Jiddu Krishnamurti put it: *Without first knowing yourself, how can you know that which is true? Illusion is inevitable without self-knowledge.*

More than anything I wanted to know myself so that I could heal my wounds. So I body-slammed, power-bombed, and pile-drove the hell out of my ego like I was a Total Diva in the World Wrestling Entertainment industry. And more often than not the ego won, and I'd become a bratty showoff chasing after an impossible dream that had my name in big, bright lights.

One of my first features helped me recognize my limitations. It was about young children who were being sold by their parents to work as camel jockeys in the United Arab Emirates (UAE). A camel jockey is someone who rides a camel during a race, and in the UAE races, the riders are typically young children that are starved by their caretakers because the lighter the rider is, the faster the camel can run. Some children are actually *glued* to the camels to ensure they don't fall off during the race.

Young children have worked as camel jockeys in the countries of the Persian Gulf for hundreds of years. According to a 2005 report by Anti Slavery, a British nongovernmental organization, hundreds of children are trafficked to the UAE to work as camel jockeys each year. The majority of the boys come from Sudan, Pakistan, Bangladesh, and Mauritania.

For this story, Bushra and I went to a home in a suburb of Khartoum called Kalakla. It belonged to Abdelrazig, a father who'd sold his two boys, 10-year-old Omer and 14-year-old Mazin, to a female trafficker when they were younger. They'd both worked in the UAE for two years after their mother died from malaria, and then returned home. When we arrived at their small shack, the power was out and we had to conduct the interviews by candlelight.

"I didn't understand what was happening at the time," Omer told us. He was petite for his age with a round, expressionless face. It was obvious from his body language that he was uncomfortable with the topic. "I was scared to be away from my home."

I shot Abdelrazig a nasty look. *How could you do this to your children?* I'd made up my mind that he was a jerk-off parent harming his little boys for money.

*Who does that?* I scoffed.

Bushra asked the boys about their salary and living conditions in the UAE and Mazin responded that their salary had been paid to their parents. They'd slept in stables with several other children on beds of hay. Mazin said that if Omer fell off the camel, he'd be beaten by one of the workers.

"I didn't get beaten because I made sure to stay on," he explained. Like Omer, Mazin's face was without any emotion in the soft yellow glow.

Camel jockeying is one of the worst forms of child labor that has ever been reported. Children who survive are emotionally scarred and ill-equipped to return to their families. In an interview with a representative of Save the Children, I was told that the children lost interest in living out their lives once they returned. They showed signs of severe depression and trauma. Omer and Mazin were prime examples of this.

"There is nothing good about this experience," Omer jumped in. "I don't like to think about it and I will try never to remember it."

Wearing my judgmental eyes, I came to a conclusion: Abdelrazig was a very bad man, right up there with Omar al-Bashir. This was the story I'd type up for IRIN. I jotted down a few notes and glared at him out of the corner of my eye. Sensing my hostility, Abdelrazig jumped up and began to speak aggressively in Arabic.

"We had no money and I could find no way to work! If these boys do not work, then they do not get fed. Would you rather that they die?" He had a candle in his hand. I noticed in the lowlight that he looked more desperate than anything. Perhaps there was more to this story and he wasn't a heartless father after all.

*Ego wins again! Self-awareness: LOSER.* I wrote down.

After further investigation I discovered that most of the families involved in this type of trafficking were of a nomadic tribe called Rashaida. They originated from the Hejaz region of Saudi Arabia but now resided mostly near Sudan's eastern borders. Camel racing was a big part of Middle Eastern culture and a widely accepted sport. As a descendant of this poor tribe, Abdelrazig had been sold by *his* parents to work as a camel jockey in the UAE. Due to limited resources, it had become a cultural norm carried forward without question because they were all stuck in survival mode. Abdelrazig wanted to ensure that at the very least, his boys wouldn't starve to death under his care.

Through this experience I saw that I was projecting the unprocessed issues I had with my own parents onto Abdelrazig and his boys. At this stage of my life, I still believed that everything was their fault, including my alcohol addiction. Of course, nothing could be further from the truth. But I had a long way to go in my own spiritual evolution, which was okay. Life was a process. I could get up and try to be more self-aware with the next story.

Emotionally, mentally, and spiritually, I wanted to *wake up*.

***

Another story I'll never forget was about Sudan's tea ladies—the women who sit curbside on Khartoum's city streets and sell tiny cups of tea from small boxes nestled between their legs. The tea ladies are constantly running or hiding from the government for participating in petty trade, prohibited under Section 20 of the Khartoum State Public Order Act. The punishment for anyone convicted of violating this act is a fine, a possible jail term, and twenty-five lashes. IRIN let me know I'd be the first person to write about this situation in years, so I took the job with utmost seriousness. There was limited paperwork on the subject, so it entailed a ton of fieldwork.

The main problem is that the ladies can't afford the licensing or medical inspection required to sell the tea. In order to get set up properly, they needed to buy the ingredients to make the tea, as well as pay a license fee of 5,000 dinars ($20). They are also required to undergo medical tests to prove they are free of contagious diseases. The medical certificate costs another 5,500 dinars. The tea vendors must also be able to provide proof of residency and pay a garbage collection fee of an additional 5,000 dinars a month. The cost of all those requirements is colossal for someone who can only, at the best of times, make $120 a month (which, oddly enough, was almost the exact amount BES was paying me).

On a discreet street in Emina el Bahri, a small town near Khartoum, Bushra and I sat with Sada, a young woman—probably twenty-seven—on the porch of a small shop that sold knickknacks and syrupy sweets. After a long workday, Sada said she made only four dollars and she used this to feed her four children.

"This life is very difficult. But what can I do? There is no other way for me to make money," she explained. Since her husband left for Darfur two years ago, she had been the sole provider, and she worked from early morning to late evening seven days a week.

The streets of Khartoum and surrounding areas are filled with women who sell tea in the doorways of local shops, behind buildings, and under trees. Most of them are internally displaced, uprooted from their homes, or refugees from neighboring war-torn countries. Some have been divorced or widowed, and, due to lack of education, selling tea is their only source of income.

"The police come and take all of my tools. They take my pot, stools, and spoons, and destroy them," Sada said.

After half a dozen interviews and more than a dozen cups of tea loaded—and I mean *loaded*—with sugar, I felt that something was off (and no, it wasn't about a sugar buzz). The tea ladies were acting strange with me.

"Bushra! What's the real story man? I feel like you're holding out." In the back of our UN truck, we sat side by side and I dabbed at my forehead to remove blobs of dusty sweat. Bushra sighed, finally ready to let the cat out of the bag.

"Okay, okay. The tea is a ruse—it's *aragy* they sell."

*Aragy* is Sudanese hooch, an alcoholic gin made from dates. It is illegally made and brewers thrive despite Sharia, which means it is very easy to get your hands on as long you have the right connections. But if you get caught peddling, consuming, or purchasing it, the punishment is forty lashes.

"Bushra! Why are you only telling me this now?" I asked, astonished.

*"Ma tasa'alni."* He shrugged. *Don't ask me.*

I gave him a look.

*"Ana baha-zer!"* He smiled sheepishly. *I'm kidding!*

Back into the field we went, but this time to broach the subject of *aragy*, which only a few women were willing to admit to selling. They said they had no shame in this because, again, it was all about survival. They had to feed their kids.

"The only way to avoid the fines is to run!" one lady, swathed in a marvelous *tobe*, told me. She had a mischievous smile on her face as if it were a game. I asked her if she was scared of the police, and in response she threw back her head and gave a hearty laugh. She could handle them, she told me.

*"Ma muskilla!"* she chortled, smiling.

I thoroughly enjoyed interviewing the tea ladies. They had feisty, rambunctious spirits—how I saw myself—and so I'd developed a bit of a bias towards them. I wanted to write in a way that would exonerate them, and, of course, point my finger at the Sudanese government. Why were they being chased around town? They are sweet, innocent mothers for crying out loud! But Bushra pointed out that even though the women were the underdogs, they were still breaking the law.

He was right, and I thanked him for reminding me to write a well-balanced story, minus my favoritism.

At times I'd turn in a 4,500-word story to IRIN only to have it cut down to 1,200. I overdid it intentionally because I needed to know that I'd provided all the facts. I let IRIN decide from there what was relevant and what wasn't. I wanted to aim for the *true story* as Erich had requested back in Kenya, regardless of IRIN's censorship. I never knew how the edit would go, but I learned not to take the final decision personally. Erich would usually email me a quick explanation:

*Shannon,*

*As a part of the UN system, IRIN complies with overall UN decisions on reporting internal matters, therefore:*

- *It is editorial policy not to pre-empt or report on the content of contentious UN Security Council resolutions that may have serious political and security implications.*

- *Not to use or quote material from leaked UN documents and reports ahead of their publication, even when other news agencies have done so. Not to use or quote material from internal UN meetings and briefings.*

Unlike William, he wouldn't call me up to make sure I understood. No, Erich's communication was always strategic. He left it up to me to work out the details and didn't worry about sparing my feelings. So I'd respond with a simple "noted" and work out the rest in my own time.

***

Unity High School was *intense* compared to BES. Lesson-planning required a lot more structure, and going from a classroom of fourteen kids to nearly thirty was like cruising in a Volkswagen bug down a country back road before hopping on a four-loop roller coaster while sitting backwards. Trying to reign them all in at the same time was a daunting task. The noise in the room was so loud that at times it felt as if I were losing my mind. As soon as I got one side of the room quiet, the other side would erupt in giggles or someone would have to tattle on someone else, and then everyone would have to put in their two cents.

I was an unconventional teacher. One of the things I invented was a cake contest. The kids were supposed to take ownership of the ingredients and design. (I was picturing outrageous kid formations.) But on the day of the contest they arrived with immaculate creations that one might see on TLC's television show *Cake Boss*. I didn't know whether to scold their parents or have a laugh, but I did know that we couldn't let so many marvelous cakes go to waste.

Imagining I was dressed up in a Victorian gown, beehive wig, and a ghastly corset, I declared: "Let us eat cake!"

Sometimes the lessons got out of hand and I got into trouble with Alfie's administrative assistant, Rupert. Rupert didn't like me all that much. According to him, my teaching style wasn't up to par with Unity's standards.

How *could* it be? I'd never had any proper training. I was just flying by the seat of my pants. Translation: Rupert's worst nightmare.

One day he called me into his office, where he was waiting for me with his arms folded across his chest and a stern look on his face. I didn't feel nervous at all. I knew he'd be hard-pressed to fire me in the middle of a school year. Who would replace me?

"I got an interesting call from Zara's father the other day," he started.

Rupert's humongous nose was covered by the most swollen, puss-filled zits I'd ever seen. The zit situation made it really hard to concentrate on his words whenever one was engaged in a one-on-one with him.

"What did he say?" I asked. *Look at his eyes, Shan. Not his nose. His eyes! His eyes!*

I looked at his nose. *Doh!* I mentally slapped my forehead.

"He said you've been telling scary stories to the class and Zara isn't sleeping at night. She's having nightmares and is refusing to sleep in her room."

I grimaced. *Busted.*

For the last few weeks I had indeed been telling spooky tales to the class, and each day the kids begged me to do it. I had no idea it was having a negative effect on anyone. I used our long, spacious chalkboard and boxes of colored chalk to draw pictures for added affect. The story was about a class trip to The Haunted Forest, where one by one the students slowly began to disappear without a trace. In the story the kids didn't know yet what was happening. All they knew was that there was a mysterious man living in the forest without a face and an ax...

Okay, it was probably a bit much for most kids. But I grew up in a house where scary stories were a fun way to spend quality time with family. My parents told us that our house had been built over a graveyard and there wasn't enough money to dig up the bodies so the builders plopped the house on top. As a result, we had a Green Hand living with us. Sometimes the Green Hand would take our food, but other than that it was pretty friendly!

"Oops! Sorry about that. It won't happen again," I promised Rupert. Later that day I decided to give the story an ending so my students would no longer ask me to tell it.

"It turns out the disappearing kids had discovered a secret land through a mysterious door in one of the forest trees. The land was made out of their favorite foods..."

"Like crisps and baklava?" asked Walid, a husky kid with thick black curls.

"Yes! Everything they could imagine. And guess who the faceless guy was? It was Miss Shannon wearing an invisible mask!" Taking cues from Disney, I told them that in the end they all lived happily ever after.

***

In other news, I was the proud owner of a pet chicken. This happened randomly while on my way to the *suk* one evening for *aysh, jabanah, suker, laban,* and *moya.* On the walk over I stopped to admire a truck filled with chicks. The driver, a Muslim man wearing a dirt-stained *jellabiya* and *taggia* (Muslim cap) was smoking a Bringi, a brand of cigarettes produced by Haggar Cigarette & Tobacco Company in Khartoum.

"*Ahlan, salam aleikum. Masa al khair. Kaef?*" He extended his hand and I shook it.

"*Masa al noor. Kaef?*" We greeted one another for several long minutes, and then the driver asked, "*Mumkin assaid?*" *Can I help you?*

I didn't know how to say "I was just adoring your cute, little baby chickens" in Arabic, so I said, "*Haba haba! Haloa shadid!*" *Little! Very beautiful!*

In typical Sudanese fashion, the driver grabbed a chick from the back and placed it in my hands so I could admire one up close.

"*Inti haloa shadid.*" The driver thought I was beautiful. I smiled at the compliment. "*Beddek?*" *You want?*

I shook my head and said no, thank you. It was a nice gesture, but what would I do with a baby chicken?

As I pet the bird's fuzzy yellow head, I didn't notice that the driver had hopped back into his truck and started to pull away.

"*Shinu? Istanna! Marsha wen?*" I shouted after him.

The driver popped his head out the window and gave me a wide, toothless grin, "*Inti haloa shadid!*" And then he was gone.

*Holy crap! What am I going to do now?*

I certainly couldn't leave it there on the side of the road to be devoured by the street dogs. He'd be dead in no time. This meant I'd have to take him home, but where would I put him? How would I feed him? I didn't have a backyard and I knew very little about birds except that they were supposed to have little bird brains and eat seeds and worms.

As I walked home I held the bird gently in my arms and stared curiously. Lately, I'd been isolating myself from everything but work and school. A fuzzy yellow friend would do me some good. But I'd have to be careful not to let anybody find out. Unity might just fire me over this one.

When I arrived at my apartment, I sat the bird on my bed and said, "I'm going to name you Fred."

Fred chirped.

Fred's brain was anything but small, and he had a huge heart. He grew attached to me the same way a child attaches to its mother. He'd follow me all around the house, and while I worked on my laptop he'd cuddle at my side or jump all over the keyboard and delete rows of important research. I can't tell you how many times I thanked God for the undo button.

In the mornings Fred would follow me into the bathroom and jump into the shower so he could be closer to me, and then he'd get freaked out by the water and jump out, only to jump back in again, and then out, and then in again. I called this behavior his chicken dance, and every morning it was the same routine.

"Oh, Fred," I'd say and scoop him into a towel to dry him off while planting a kiss on his fluffy, wet forehead.

Fred chirped.

\*\*\*

It was a hot Saturday in December. Christmas was just around the corner and I'd been spending so much of my free time in the field that I hardly noticed. It was blazing hot and hardly felt like Christmastime. I had spent the morning at Mygoma orphanage, where 400 children had been abandoned by young and unmarried mothers because they were afraid of being condemned by Islamic law, which didn't allow sexual intercourse before marriage. I nestled into the couch to write up a story. Bundled in a towel, Fred dozed serenely at my side.

As I tried to focus on the kids in the orphanage, my thoughts kept drifting off topic and onto the subject of what it meant to be a professional writer. Since IRIN had such a powerful publishing platform, my words had the ability to heal or harm, inspire or destroy, and in a *big way*. I wanted my stories to help the Sudanese overcome their issues and reach their potential, and this is where I felt unclear about IRIN's intentions—and the media machine on the whole. IRIN's approach to writing felt very cookie-cutter. Basically I had to start each story with a disheartening visual of the crisis at hand, and then follow with an equally depressing quote. I looked down at what I was writing. My Mygoma story started like this:

*Musa's mother abandoned him in the arms of Sudanese policemen months ago when he was only two weeks old. The police took him to Mygoma, a small orphanage on a dusty street in Dem, a town three miles south of the Sudanese capital, Khartoum.*

*Rose, a child psychologist at Mygoma, described how Musa was hard-hit by the separation from his mother. She said: "He would not eat, he would not sleep. He did not want to interact even though we tried to convince him and give him special care."*

*After only two weeks at the orphanage, Musa died. According to Rose, he died of a broken heart.*

Starting a story this way was all about creating an emotional appeal—I got that. But for me a scene like this stirred up emotions of sadness and helplessness. I wanted to write in a way that *empowered* both the Sudanese *and* the readers.

I had read that Mahatma Gandhi, who took journalism very seriously, was once the editor of three English weeklies. He said, "Journalism, to be useful and serviceable to the country, will take its definite place only when it becomes unselfish and when it devotes its best for the service of the country."

Gandhi believed that the sole aim of journalism should be service.

Writing as a form of service. What an intriguing concept. I'd always wanted to contribute to the world in some capacity. Members of twelve-step groups are passionate about providing peer support to people who are desperately trying to overcome their addictions. Mormons always show up for members or non-members living in their ward boundaries. In times of crisis, they drop everything and make meals for one another and care for each other's kids. Muslims are zealous about charity and feeding the poor.

What if I could figure out a way to be of service through the written word? Maybe I could figure out how to empower people who were like me, struggling with alcohol and drug addiction.

Yawning, I stretched out my legs (carefully, so as not to stir Fred). In a couple of weeks, I'd be in Darfur to cover a story for the UN Population Fund alongside some of the most powerful journalists in the business. I was curious to know if after so many years in this profession these well-known journalists had figured out a way to keep their egos in check and their issues at bay so they didn't bleed into the written word. Did they see their work as a form of service? And if so, what did that look like and how could I make it happen in my life today—within IRIN's format? I was excited for the chance to ask these questions and witness seasoned journalists in action in a true crisis setting.

But if I'd known then what I was about to experience, I probably would have stayed in Khartoum. As a naïve girl from Utah, I wasn't prepared and didn't have the capacity to deal with any of it. It was unlike anything I had ever experienced, not even in Khartoum or Kibera. Like a poltergeist with an endless gaping mouth, piercing howl, and hollowed out eyes, Darfur would haunt me for years.

# Chapter 10

*In less than an hour I would board a small plane headed for Darfur.*

The plane had been chartered by the United Nations Population Fund (UNFPA), and our trip would be led by a woman who would one day hire me to write for UNFPA's Humanitarian Response Unit in New York City. I'll call her Kim. Kim was the Chief of Humanitarian Response for UNFPA in Sudan, and she wanted me to come so I could highlight a concert UNFPA was hosting for thousands of internally displaced persons (IDPs) living in Otash camp near Nyala, the capital of South Darfur. Approximately the size of Spain, Darfur is divided into five federal states: South Darfur, North Darfur, East Darfur, West Darfur and Central Darfur.

UNPFA had been mandated to initiate gender-based violence (GBV) prevention and treatment programs in Darfur, implement measures to protect women and girls, and build the capacity of UN agencies, government institutions, and non-governmental organizations. The concert would be held in honor of the international 16 Days of Activism against Gender Violence campaign, which was held annually. The campaign originated in

1991 and since its inception has grown exponentially. This year, campaign activities would take place in 130 countries.

In Darfur, violence against women was a big, ugly ordeal. In March, Médecins Sans Frontières (MSF) reported that between October 2004 and mid-February 2005, MSF doctors in Darfur treated almost 500 women and girls who had been raped. Almost one-third of the victims had been raped more than once by a single or multiple perpetrators, and 81 percent reported being attacked by armed militia. MSF believed these statistics reflected only a fraction of the total number of victims because many women and girls were reluctant to report the crime or seek treatment.

But the Sudanese government refuted these findings. According to state record, only five cases of rape had actually been prosecuted and just three of those ended in convictions. It was becoming common knowledge just how corrupt Sudan's government really was. A secret list drawn up by a UN-appointed commission of inquiry into the Darfurian conflict had recently named fifty-one war crime suspects, including senior government and military officials, militia and rebel leaders, and foreign army officers.

In 2008, the International Criminal Court's top prosecutor would call for the arrest of President Bashir for genocide, crimes against humanity, and war crimes in Darfur. This appeal was the first-ever request by the ICC for the arrest of a current head of state. Sudan rejected the indictment, leading Bashir's old enemy Turabi to dare Bashir to turn himself into The Hague (the seat of Dutch government, where the ICC is based) and face the charges. The challenge resulted in another arrest for Turabi by Bashir. In 2009, the ICC issued an arrest warrant for Bashir stating that the looting and destruction of villages in Darfur was not only tolerated by government officials, but also systematically organized with troops and militia members allowed to take whatever they wanted, including livestock and other civilian property, after killing, raping, and torturing tens of thousands of people.

It seemed strange that we were going to throw a musical concert in the middle of all of this. I had asked Kim about this when she'd first invited me.

"To celebrate," Kim explained.

I gave her a look. "What are we celebrating exactly?"

"Life. Music. Dancing."

She explained that this event was important because it was the first time since 2003 (when the crisis began) that the Darfurians would gather as a community for something *positive*.

"Typically refugees and IDPs don't have access to cultural activities like music, dance, poetry, or drama, and not having these things contributes to their sense of isolation from the rest of society. We're bringing some of their all-time favorite musicians and artists to let them know that they're not forgotten and that their lives are worth celebrating."

Among the artists, UNFPA had invited Abdel Abdelrazig el Kabli, an internationally renowned Sudanese singer, along with Sudanese singers Samia Dunia and Abdel Gadir Salim. As Kim explained in further detail, my mind flashed back to my early teen years when I'd discovered a wide-mouthed Steven Tyler draped in colorful scarfs and raven black hair. He was singing in Aerosmith's video "Cryin'" and I remember thinking he was the most erotic, peculiar, and passionate beast-of-a-man I'd ever seen. I'd promptly spent my teenage years obsessing over his every move while getting lost in his music.

Today, Tyler inspires me more than ever. He's a well-known recovery advocate and speaks out about his addiction struggles in order to spread the message of hope. Although he sings on stage for tens of thousands of people, in 2014, he stood before eleven Maui Drug Court graduates and their families.

"I'm nervous here because I'm telling you all my truth," he said. "I am also a drug addict and alcoholic and fighting it every day."

If it weren't for Tyler's music, I wouldn't have known or cared about his recovery story, which has given me inspiration to speak out publicly regarding my own struggles.

"Wow," I said to Kim. "What a cool idea."

Kim was like a sunrise: bright and warm. She even had vibrant carrot-colored hair to match her luminous demeanor. I imagined she was her high school's number one cheerleader overflowing with endless amounts of optimism and energy. Her dedication to her work reminded me a lot of other UN workers I'd met in Khartoum who were sincerely trying to make a difference with their programs despite the political hoops they had to jump through. Kim honestly believed in UNFPA's work and the people in her care.

"We're going to have an amazing time," she said sunnily.

Right before the flight to Nyala, our group of national and international journalists, UN staff, and Sudanese entertainers gathered for a delicious meal of hummus, *full*, *tamia*, and *injera*, a sourdough-risen Ethiopian flat bread. While everyone talked excitedly, I hid in a corner with my plate and face-stuffed to the max. I was fretful about going and was hoping the hummus would somehow placate my woes. I had been trying to get to Darfur for months now, and even had a few trips previously planned. But something had always fallen through at the last minute. Now the moment was finally here, and I wasn't so sure it was a good idea. When I'd told my parents that I was going to Sudan, I'd said:

"Dad, Sudan is more than one million square miles. The civil war and genocide are *very* far away from Khartoum. There's no need to worry."

There was no way I could've known that a year and a half later I'd be boarding a plane to Darfur in order to witness the genocide first-hand and sell stories about it to the UN. This trip meant a lot to a girl who'd once been labeled a rebel, a lush, and a stoner. I thought back to that girl and her desperate attempts to find her unique purpose in a big, noisy world, and I couldn't help but feel that in some way seeing Darfur was the reason I'd come.

But what did that *mean*?

Since I'd been oblivious during the coup and the riots, I wanted to ensure this didn't happen again. I had purposely been studying about Darfur for several months just in case I ever got to go. I knew exactly what the dangers were. Unlike the police force in Khartoum, Darfur's government-backed militia was not afraid of foreigners. Aid workers were raped, murdered, and kidnapped the same as civilians. But seeing Darfur was an opportunity I couldn't pass up. During the riots, I'd arrived after most of the chaos had been quelled, and all my other feature stories had been about situations past. I wanted to experience a crisis up close and personal so that I could connect more deeply with the people I was writing about. In general, I still suffered from an inability to form attachments to people or things, and as a result I always felt disconnected to my stories. I hoped Darfur would break the shatterproof armor I'd built around myself and help me connect to my own vulnerabilities.

"Excuse me?" A man's voice interrupted my thoughts.

I covered my mouth to hide the massive spoonful of baba ganoush I'd just shoved into it and whirled around to face him.

"Hi," I said as a chunk of tomato flew out. (I am a messy eater; so sue me.)

"What are you doing here?"

The man was the epitome of tall, dark, and handsome. He was also Australian, and like a sucker for a sugary, gooey pastry, I was also a sucker for a foreign accent. If only I didn't feel that he was questioning my intelligence and my right to be present with these important people, I probably would've flirted with him.

"Excuse me?" I asked, posed for a fight.

"I don't mean to be a jerk. But I've been doing this a really long time and you—" he paused to look me up and down. "You don't belong here."

I used to get this a lot, and I blamed it on my massive chubster-cheeks because they made me look like I was twelve.

"Listen—"

"No. *You* listen. You can't be part of this business and not be affected by what you see. I don't care who you are. You want to be a big shot and go to Darfur? Fine. But what you're about to see will change you. *Forever.* Ask yourself: is it worth it?"

His name was Randy and he knew what he was talking about. Randy had been one of the few journalists who'd made it into Rwanda during the 1994 genocide that left over 600,000 people dead. He told me that the pilot refused to land in Rwanda because of the danger and that instead he'd hovered the plane low enough for Randy and his partner to jump.

"It was too dark outside, so we couldn't see very well, and we jumped out into a pile of dead, bloody bodies."

I frowned at him. "I appreciate it, but I'm not the sort of person to go off someone else's experience, and I'm already committed. I'm going. I'll be fine."

Randy shook his head. Perhaps he saw me as his younger self and he wanted to protect me in a way nobody had protected him before he became a big shot in the business. As one last effort to convince me to stay, he said, "It's not seeing the dead that will destroy you. It's the smell of death *in the living* as they rot in the displaced camps that will haunt you every day for the rest of your life."

We stared into each other's eyes for a brief moment.

Twenty minutes later, Kim signaled that it was time to board and we got on a plane and flew southwest to Nyala.

\*\*\*

When we landed, the first order of business was attending a security briefing to discuss proper protocol and danger zones. The UN security team in Darfur crammed our noisy group into a tiny office that had a large map of Darfur on one wall. I pushed my way to the front so I could see it more clearly. It had bright red, orange, and yellow swirls around various cities and valleys.

"There are very few areas in South Darfur that are completely safe. Proposed 'safe areas' have threatened to consolidate the ethnic cleansing taking place here. However, the yellow areas on this map are more civilized than others and supported by UN staff."

"What about the red zones?" I asked. Blood-red marker was everywhere.

"The red indicates an active war zone. These areas have been taken over by the *Janjaweed* and should be avoided at all costs." The security guy paused and looked around to ensure he had everyone's attention.

"There will be a handful of AMIS peacekeepers that'll accompany you while you're here, but as you know, they are not allowed to carry guns. You'll need to travel with extreme caution."

"How are they supposed to keep us safe?" asked an Ethiopian woman named Ruth who worked for the United Nations Development Fund for Women (UNIFEM). Her question was met with an uneasy silence.

In 2004, the AMIS (African Union Mission in Sudan) peacekeeping force was established with 150 Rwandan troops. It quickly became apparent that 150 troops weren't enough, so they were joined by 150 Nigerian troops. By the time I got to Darfur in December 2005, this number had increased to 3,300. The troops worked closely with the UN Mission in Sudan as the only external military force in Darfur until it was replaced by UNAMID, a hybrid peacekeeping mission created by the African Union and United Nations. Currently, it's the largest peacekeeping mission in the world.

"Another important point is that no person in this room is to capture faces or names for a story. If the government finds that these people have given us any information, they will be killed without question. Is that understood?"

We all nodded.

After the briefing, Kim suggested we stop by a craft sale on our way to the hotel in order to provide financial support to the Darfurian women who were desperate for ways to feed their families. We hopped into one of the six UN vehicles supplied for our trip. Next to me sat Ingrid, a pretty young blond from the Norwegian Embassy. In the back were Abdul, a Lebanese journalist, and Ruth from UNIFEM. Kim sat next to the driver. We cruised deliberately through Nyala's lively streets, which looked like close copies of Khartoum's.

"Okay! Okay!" the street kids ran after us with friendly waves, bright smiles, and dirt plastered on their faces and clothes.

"Okay! Okay!" we shouted back from behind the rolled up windows of our air-conditioned vehicle.

Once out of the city we began our descent into the desert, which appeared to be a mash-up of a post-apocalyptic wasteland and the prehistoric world. There was a desolate, predatory vibe and it clung to our vehicle like a vampire leech sucking the life from us. There was something else in the atmosphere, too, but I couldn't quite put my finger on it.

As I searched for the right words, I noticed everyone in the SUV had gone quiet—very unusual for our bunch. The only noise came from the air conditioner that blasted from the front dash at full speed in order to counteract the heat. Outside the window, glowing sunrays electrified the desert floor, making it appear as if it were on fire. In the distance I could see dinosaur-sized camels moving up and down on the horizon, and I sensed there was a T-Rex lurking somewhere close by and that he was hungry.

Finally Kalma camp—the largest IDP camp in Darfur with a population of roughly 155,000—came into view.

"Oh my God," Ingrid whispered.

The camp was laid out in well-ordered rows of huts shaped like miniature igloos. Each hut was constructed of various forms of decomposing trash plastered strategically over branches and twigs. I could hardly believe that human beings lived *on* this malevolent strip of land, let alone *inside* these filthy contraptions. I had read somewhere that the rains had fallen above the region's average this year, and that every time the rain fell it wiped out the camp homes and the owners had to gather the soggy trash.

"Let's get out and have a look around," Kim suggested from the front seat.

Suddenly we were two disobedient teenagers. Ingrid and I shook our heads.

*Get out? Here? Is she crazy?*

I couldn't remember what color this area was on the map, but it sure didn't feel like any zone I wanted to explore. I felt again the sensation of being watched. I wanted to point this out to Kim, but she was the veteran and I was the newbie. Surely, she knew best.

"Come on," Kim nudged as she hopped out of the car. "It will help you get a feel for camp life."

Ingrid and I looked at each other.

"Ladies, this is why you came, isn't it?" Ruth said from the back seat, and then she hopped out with Abdul.

We sat for a few more seconds, and then I took a deep breath and pushed the door open. The sun greeted me like a semi-truck greets a dawdling rabbit in the highway. I doubled over to catch

my breath. Darfur's heat felt much worse than Khartoum's—
perhaps because there wasn't a spot of shade in sight. I tried
looking ahead to see where everyone had wandered, but the sun
was blinding. It began to broil the top layer of my skin and I
cussed myself out for forgetting the sunscreen.

Where did everyone go? Even Ingrid had disappeared. The
camp seemed deserted except for two young children running up
and down one of the walkways. Instinctively, I wanted to run up
and scold them for playing irresponsibly in this hazardous area,
as if it were a radioactive waste disposal site and they'd snuck
in underneath a barbed wire fence. But this was their *home*. I
shuddered. All of a sudden, I put my finger on what was in the
atmosphere that I couldn't put my finger on earlier. It was the
*energy,* and there was really only one word to describe it: *evil.*
It wasn't a post-apocalyptic-prehistoric mash up. Darfur was on
a whole new planet from a whole new galaxy I'd never heard
of. It was ruled by a murderous sun and had its own breed of
ferocious, gnarly-toothed creatures that stalked prey from murky
shadows unforeseen. For my sake, I hoped the creatures only
came out at night.

But what about the kids? The contrast of them frolicking in
this desert wasteland was striking.

*Where is everybody?*

I had been standing too long and began to feel extremely
lightheaded. Better to move around in this heat. I walked over to
a deserted row and poked my head inside one of the huts to get
a better look.

"Oh!" I jumped back, startled. Inside was a woman wrapped
in a golden *tobe* so that she blended in perfectly with the sand.
She was sitting on a stool and making a cup of tea.

*"Fudul,"* she said kindly.

She gestured for me to join her on a small stool. There was
hardly any room for her to sit inside comfortably, let alone the

both of us. Conflicted, I looked around for the others. These families had very little food; I couldn't let her waste some of it on my bloated gut. Then again, hospitality meant a lot to Sudanese women, and I doubt they had much opportunity to host anybody here.

"*La shukran,*" I said, trying to soften my refusal with a kind smile.

"*Fudul,*" she said again.

I didn't see how I could possibly sit and have a cup of tea with this woman while pretending that our lives weren't in danger. What would I do after we were done? Get up and leave her here while I went back to safety in my air-conditioned car?

"*La shukran,*" I said again. My face felt like it was blistering. I needed shade. *Fast.*

"*Lematha?*" she asked. She wanted to know why.

As I searched for the right words to explain my dilemma, both in English and in Arabic, my eyes searched her face. She looked as if she were a thousand years old. Her skin was leathery from the sun and she had deep scars etched into her cheeks. I wondered what they were from. Suddenly the woman's face tightened; the hairs on the back of my neck stood up. I heard the sound of hooves striking sand. Something was rushing toward me.

I braced myself as I whirled around to see four camels moving in on us. I squinted—were those people sitting on their backs?

"*Janjaweed!*" the woman yelled. *Devils on horseback.*

"Let's go!" Kim shouted from somewhere nearby. She was running. I whirled back around to face the woman once again and our eyes met. Electricity shot through me as I felt her vulnerability.

"Shannon! Car! *Now!*" Kim shouted.

"*Ana asif,*" I said, staring into her pleading eyes. *I'm sorry.*

Then I ran with my feet and heart pounding. I jumped in the vehicle and slammed the door shut. Ingrid hopped in moments later breathing deeply. Abdul was in the back. We were still waiting on Kim and Ruth.

"Did you see anything? What's out there?" Ingrid asked.

I pointed in the direction of the camels and the men. They were much closer now and I could see the outlines of guns dangling from their tan shoulders.

"What about the mom and her kids?" I asked, my voice thick with emotion. I cleared my throat to cover up that I was on the verge of tears.

Kim jumped in after Ruth and yelled, "Let's go!" Helplessly, I watched as the creatures closed in on the woman and her home.

"Wait! Stop! We can't just leave them here!" Ingrid swore.

But that's exactly what we did.

\*\*\*

We spent the night in a dusty, hot hotel and the next afternoon we were headed back into the desert, but this time to cover a particular story: displaced women who had to venture outside of their camps for firewood to cook the food provided by humanitarian agencies, so their families could eat. Their journey to find wood consisted of a three-to five-mile walk one way through thorny bushes and boulder-strewn terrain with the heavy threat of rape and abduction by both the *Janjaweed* and government militias (accused of turning their guns on civilians instead of protecting them).

"We're going into a war zone. Please prepare yourselves," the driver warned.

We were a ways into the desert by then, and with each turn of the tires my apprehension increased. Our old crew was back together: Kim, Ruth, Abdul, and Ingrid, who was seated at my side. This is how she and I had been throughout the trip, sealed together like two gel batteries. We were the only ones in the group who had never been in a war zone before, and we were white-knuckling it the whole way through.

It had been an intense morning. We had gotten up early so we could go back into the camps and conduct research and interviews with young girls about their experiences of rape. We'd sat as a group across from them in a makeshift school provided by UNICEF, and as they shared their horrific experiences, we'd sat taking notes. The experience felt highly impersonal and invasive, but we had stories to publish. I ignored my feelings and unease to do what I'd been hired to do. This would be my mantra in Darfur, I told myself: I'd go home and try to figure it all out once I was somewhere safe—like beside Fred in his towel bed on the couch—and could think more clearly. Besides, I wasn't feeling well. My skin was badly burnt and I couldn't stop thinking about the mom and the two kids we'd left behind. What had happened to them? As usual, my imagination was rich and I hated the images it was conjuring. The little family reminded me of the ants from the sidewalks of my childhood that I'd vowed to protect. Back then, I'd taken the time to pick them up and move them out of harm's way. But what had I done for this family? I understood that we couldn't pick up all these people from the desert and fly them home with us, but how could we stand there and watch them suffer? It was an impossible conundrum that I was desperate to find the answer too.

Was there another way?

"There! There!" Abdul shouted, pointing at the dark figure of a woman sitting beneath a blackened tree. It twisted toward the malicious sun with curved and serrated limbs. Our convoy stopped. Like a SWAT team, everyone jumped into action. Within minutes, cameras and microphones were out and in place. I moved to the back of the vehicle to grab my equipment.

*Camera...check.*

*Voice recorder...check.*

*Battery...um...where is my battery?*

I found it impossible to function properly in this heat. I huffed impatiently and dabbed at the dew on my forehead. By the time I found it and made my way to where the crowd had gathered, our translator was busy asking questions. I focused my camera on the scruffy woman sitting before me. She was probably eighty years old. Like the woman in the hut, she had horizontal and vertical scars carved into her face. I had learned this painful-looking mutilation was a tribal marking meant to signify beauty. At her feet sat a pile of branches and on her neck hung slabs of smooth rock on a string.

"Have you guys started in about the GBV? What'd she say?" I asked from behind my camera, repositioning myself to get a better view.

"Shannon! A few more steps and you'll be in my way," Randy scolded. He was representing UN TV and had a giant video camera in his hand. I backed up in search of a new angle.

"Look at her," Ingrid said. "She doesn't want to talk about this. Can't you see it in her face?" Through the lens of my camera I could see that the woman was quivering. Her expression suggested she thought we were invaders from another planet.

"Maybe we should go," Ruth said.

"No, we need to get the story. Ask her about her experience of rape. She's been here long enough. She's probably seen a lot," Randy said.

"Let's give her an apron," suggested a UN staff member.

From the corner of my eye, I watched the UN person run to one of the SUVs and grab a white apron that read *UNFPA* in bright orange print. She came back over and handed it to the woman. The woman stared at it, alarmed, as if the apron could bite her.

I watched all this from behind my lens and realized I was hiding. The lens was a perfect shield and made it easy to pretend that this disturbing scene was unraveling on a TV screen in front of my parent's couch back in Utah instead of just five feet away.

But I'd come to connect, not to hide.

Stepping back, I lowered my camera and watched as we—the people of the "civilized world"—stuck technical gadgets and bright lights in her face. We'd only met her moments ago and yet we were interrogating her about her private traumas.

I squatted down so the woman and I were at eye-level and I reached out and drew a circle in the sand. It was hot to touch. My eyes wandered to her rock necklace and I wondered who'd made it for her. Maybe it was a gift from a loved one and it symbolized hope—one thing we all clung to in desperate situations. She noticed that I was watching her and she looked me in the eyes. Just like with the woman in the displaced camp, I felt a jolt of energy shoot through my body.

*Namaste,* I told the woman via ESP.

*Namaste* is a Sanskrit term that means "the divine light in me honors the divine light in you." It's one of my favorite phrases and I try to think of it whenever I meet someone new and want to be more conscious with them in the moment. It is a reminder that we're all equal and share a common divinity. If only I could pause the chaos around us and say this to her...but it didn't fit the mood of the moment. Our group wasn't here to connect, but to project.

"Screw you guys, I'm not doing this," Ingrid said, and stormed off with her long, blond hair bouncing behind her.

Her words killed the buzz in a matter of seconds.

"She's not going to talk anyway. Let's just go."

Back in the car, I watched the woman through my window. I wondered what her story was, what she dreamt about at night, if she'd ever been in love, and if we shared any common experiences. I knew the rate of addiction was high among impoverished people. They sniffed glue (or anything they could get their hands on) to escape their cruel reality. Perhaps we shared more than could be found on the surface.

"We shouldn't have done that. We had no right," Ingrid said, and nobody argued.

*Have you guys started in about the GBV?* My own voice echoed in my mind.

Earlier in the day, I had seen seasoned journalists sneaking behind the displaced camps with small children and families. Curious, I'd followed them and was shocked to find that they were jotting down names in their notepads and taking photos.

"What are you guys doing?" I'd asked Yasir with BBC. "Didn't you hear the security guy say that using their names and faces would put their lives in jeopardy?"

"Yes."

"Killed. He said they'd be *killed,*" I reiterated.

"Oh, stop it. Without a face or a name, there is no story. Without a story, I don't get paid and my family doesn't eat."

I knew Yasir. We were friends and had hung out in Khartoum's social circle a few times. He was a decent, smart guy. So how was it possible that he could justify doing such a thing? And although I had no intentions of using these people's names or faces for a story, I couldn't shake the feeling that I, too, was betraying their trust.

The majority of these journalists appeared to be suffering from various forms of detachment disorder; many were downright traumatized. They could no longer feel for the wounds of the people they were meant to serve because they could no longer feel their own. I got it. A few days in Darfur burned me up quicker than nearly 700 days in Khartoum. It was exhausting to continually have to contemplate potentially massive threats in a land ruled by such radical uncertainty. The term for this is "crisis fatigue," and in the case of journalists, it typically leads to hardcore burnout.

According to the Harm Limitation Principle in the Journalism Ethics and Standards, "Weight needs to be given to the negative consequences of full disclosure...." It seems a no-brainer that this would include putting lives in jeopardy in order to share stories and make money. This creates another practical and ethical dilemma for writers trying to tell the true stories of people who have no voice in the public square and are unable to tell stories themselves.

\*\*\*

It was the day of the concert and our last day in Darfur. I wasn't sure how long we'd been here. Four, five days? Minor details like the date and time were irrelevant at this point. Even years later, I couldn't entirely recall where we ate, what my hotel room looked like, or how well I slept.

All I remember is the desert, that goddamn sun, and the stories.

Earlier in the day, the UN TV crew had showed me how they tricked their cameras to make it appear as if there were dozens of books on a table when there were really only two. The segment was meant to showcase all the hard work and supplies UNICEF was providing to Darfur's children. *If they didn't buy books as mandated, what had they spent the money on? Was everything just for show with us?* Meanwhile, the Darfurians were starving to death before our very eyes while the *Janjaweed* hunted them like game.

For the first time since coming to Khartoum, I was afraid I might actually die, and not at the hands of these devils on horseback, but from a broken heart.

*Do the work now; process your feelings later,* I kept repeating to myself.

I wanted to go home to Utah, where my family was, where my worries consisted of deciding if I should finish my college degree or if I had enough time to go to the gym.

As the concert was beginning, I stuck by Kim because she was one big fireball of energy and I thought I could live vicariously through her for the moment. It was hard not to find something to be happy about around her. I wondered how she managed to see the worst of the world and still live with joy. I'd only known her a short while, but I admired her greatly. I hoped to one day be a great leader of humanitarian issues just like her.

I had been informed I could take pictures of the people at the concert since the story didn't directly out the government and it was more about raising awareness for women's rights. At first as I captured the faces of the audience members, their expressions were dismal and unresponsive, but once Kabli took the stage, the crowd erupted. He was a candid and charismatic entertainer. I captured images of him standing on a stage improvised on a dusty patch of desert and lit up by a string of silvery white lights. The Darfurians sat around the stage in groups; children were in one area, women and girls in the other. The men sat on chairs in the back.

Raising his hand to quiet the crowd, Kabli spoke gently, "This song is dedicated to our mothers, sisters, and daughters." And then he began to sing:

*Please do not cry, but tell all mothers in the neighborhood that my passing away was due to the ugly, primitive, and dangerous circumcision...that my death was due to my early marriage and childish pregnancy and I could not tolerate the inhuman pains of delivery....*

Although the words were sad, Kabli's presence boosted the crowd. After a few verses, the ladies were ululating, a long, quivering, high-pitched howl commonly used in Arab countries and Sub-Saharan Africa to express celebration. I snapped photos as statistics about GBV in Sudan rolled around in my head: female circumcision affected over 90 percent of the girls and women living in the north part of the country, and 63 percent of girls living in rural areas were forced to marry between the ages of nine and thirteen.

When Kabli's routine ended, other singers took their turns on the stage. Between each performance, actors from a Sudanese comedy group brought the audience to laughter with short comedic skits that discussed GBV issues in a fun but purposeful manner. In one of the skits, a man pretended to be at home waiting for his wife while she worked long hours selling tea to pay the bills. When she was late getting home one night, her husband beat her for being tardy. One of the actors made the beating appear pointless and silly. Then he asked,

"Why are you beating this woman when you will not get up and work yourself? The woman does this work for you." The audience members were moved by the skit's powerful message.

"This is cool, isn't it? Look at the crowd!" Kim shouted over the noise. Almost everyone was up off the ground and celebrating in some capacity.

That day, thousands of IDPs living in Otash and surrounding areas gathered to attend the concert. Within a few short hours it was over and we were packing up. Finally, it was time to leave Darfur. As we boarded the plane, everyone but Kim looked haggard. Her event had been a smashing hit, and she was blooming in the aftermath.

Midflight, before my eyes closed for the nap of the century, I noticed she was gazing out the window with a thoughtful smile on her face.

"What are you thinking about?" I asked.

She looked over at me, her eyes tired, too, but alert.

"You know, the skits and songs from today discussed issues of violence that have never been openly discussed in Sudan before. At first it seemed like everyone was in shock. But in the end I think the women listened carefully. And more importantly? I think the men listened carefully, too."

I smiled. "The future depends on what we do in the present," I quoted. "I think Gandhi said that."

\*\*\*

The cab ride from the airport to my apartment took forever. I was in a hurry to get home to Fred. I'd left him in the care of Luke, the apartment's gatekeeper, but that didn't mean I hadn't worried about him the entire trip. Luke had looked at me like I was crazy when I'd revealed my secret pet to him and asked if he could chicken-sit while I was gone. Animals are dispensable to the Sudanese; they typically feed their working animals as little as possible (because they can barely afford to feed themselves).

When the cab finally pulled up to my complex, I hopped out and opened our gate door to find Luke sitting in a chair with a surprised expression on his face.

"Luke, what's up?" I asked, alarmed.

He began speaking in Arabic while pointing to my balcony with a flustered look on his face. Then he sighed and pointed to a bush near the stairwell, which led to a basement apartment. Nervously, I peered in.

"Fred!" I exclaimed, stunned to find him in this predicament. He was shaking. "What are you doing down here? How'd you get out?"

Fred hopped out of the bush and began to run around the cobblestone walkway as if he was Chicken Little and the sky was falling. I scooped him up in my arms and planted a kiss on his forehead.

"Poor little guy." He had jumped from our two-story balcony and was shaken by the fall.

With a friendly hug, I thanked Luke for watching him and scurried up the stairs with Fred chirping rambunctiously in my arms.

Fred was particularly attached to me that night and refused to be even a few inches away from me. If I walked too fast, he'd chirp so loudly that I'd quickly slow my pace, which meant I almost stepped on him a few times. I ended up carrying him in my arms to sooth him. Once in bed, I decided to put a movie on my laptop and popped in *The Birdcage* with Robin Williams. It was one of my all-time favorite comedies, and always made me laugh. I hoped it would help drown out the images of people in Darfur who were taking up a lot of space in my head. As soon as the movie started, my eyes began to droop. Fred slept at my side.

I drifted into a tense sleep and dreamed of Arab men riding on the back of thirty-foot T-Rex. The men had guns in their arms and were aiming them at women with thick skin and little girls with pink ribbons in their hair as they collected firewood beneath Darfur's wicked sun.

Guns blasted.

Women fell into puddles of blood.

Then the girls fell, their ribbons flailing as they hit the ground.

The dinosaurs trampled over their red-soaked stomachs and squished out their intestines while the men snickered menacingly. I turned to run and found a small hut up a hill that had beaded goods dangling from it. It was the hut from the craft sale Kim had brought us to on our first day in Darfur. Off to the left I saw a familiar tent with "UNICEF" on it. I hustled inside to hide from the men and found three young children innocently coloring on a dirt floor. My heart smiled at the sight of them. They reminded me of my students. In one corner, I saw a young boy coloring alone. I walked over to him and promptly praised his work.

"That's beautiful!" I assured.

At first, his drawing looked like an abstract painting in red, tan, and black. But after looking more closely I realized I was viewing it upside down. I repositioned myself to see what the boy had really drawn: a smoking gun with airborne bullets headed in the direction of a little girl's heart. At her feet were several other children covered in blood. They were lying on his tan-colored earth, dead.

I bolted from my nightmare, a scream caught in my throat. I tried to let it out but only a strained noise came out. Something was wrong.

Fred was lying next to me with his neck twisted at an awkward angle. He wasn't breathing.

The scream escaped.

*Had I really smothered him?*

In that moment, the eight-year-old I was and the adult I had become converged: I saw a long line of all those I'd wanted to protect, my bug buddies, the kids bullied by religious dogma and hurt by their parents, my students, UAE's camel jockeys, those incarcerated in Omdurman's prison, Khartoum's tea ladies, the Darfurian children playing in the toxic wasteland that was their home, the kind woman who'd offered me tea in a tent made of trash, the woman with slabs of rock on a string around her neck, and now Fred...

*You knew better!* I accused myself.

I jumped to my feet with beads of perspiration slithering down my sunburnt skin. I fell to my knees and began to pound angrily on the mattress. I cursed the *Janjaweed*, the people I'd left behind, the selfish, no-good journalists, and *myself*. For some reason, I'd thought that I was different from the creatures lurking in that nightmarish desert. I was meant to be a people's champion and expose irrationality and abuse in order to set us all free. But instead I'd revealed an ugly, inescapable truth: I was a selfish, no-good killer, too.

My sobs heaved out of me from a place deep down; I sounded as if my heart were rupturing into a million pieces. And when there were no more tears, I lay on the floor and stared dead-eyed at the wall across from me. I don't know how long I stared at the wall, but I hung onto that moment as long as I could because I knew what came after it: I had to deal with Fred's body.

And after that, I would have to deal with what I'd witnessed in Darfur, and try and make sense of what it all meant about our world and all the people in it, including me.

\*\*\*

Soon a sunbeam peered through my window. School would start in a few hours. It was time to get up and deal with it and try to get an hour of sleep in. I pulled myself over to the bed, picked up my little friend, and cradled him in my arms. I laid him on the balcony where he would surely be eaten by the rodents and insects. It seemed like the only option.

*Put him down; process your feelings later.*

My mantra from Darfur. But I wasn't in Darfur anymore.

# Chapter 11

*T*he next morning I went to school with a smile plastered over my face. I acted as if Fred never existed, and Darfur? Oh, Darfur was just another workday out in the field. *No big deal.*

I was eight years old again, pretending.

The pain of these events was easier to suppress in the daytime because I could get lost in caring for my students or shop mindlessly at the *dukan*. But when dusk fell, the prospect of sleep terrors increased my anxiety substantially. They played on repeat like a badly scratched Halloween Hits record. Fred became a part of them. In my dreams, he was killed alongside the women and girls.

*Guns blasted.*

*My friends fell into puddles of blood.*

But it wasn't dinosaurs or the *Janjaweed* trampling over their bodies with a menacing grin.

It was me. *I* was the *killer*.

I couldn't forgive myself for what happened to Fred or for leaving the Darfurians behind. I had desperately wanted to help, but I'd been powerless and afraid. I was a big, fat failure. Now I was punishing myself with guilt so intense it just might saw me in half. I couldn't sleep; I hated being awake. Unable to take it any longer, I called up my buck-toothed, eccentric Sudanese friend who thought he was an African Prince.

"Hey Amir, can you get me some *aragy*?"

Amir said he knew a lady that sold it near my old neighborhood in Dem and he could have a bottle for me in less than an hour. I told him an hour was too long.

"Hurry," I pressed.

A little while later, I was sitting alone on my bed with a used soda bottle in my lap. The brewer had filled it with the cloudy, yellow liquid—*aragy*—and there were a few unidentifiable chunks floating in it.

*Don't do it. You've come so far. Think about tomorrow. The kids. Your work.*

"Shut it," I said bitterly, sick and tired of the chatter in my head.

When it hits the back of your throat, the burn of *aragy* is brutal. I took a shot and the warm, toxic liquid spread through my body and mind, promptly smoothing out all my edges. I let out a sigh and took another shot. All the blood and brokenness were off in the blurry distance now, but not far enough.

I guzzled the *aragy*, hard.

Less than an hour later, I was vomiting all over the bathroom floor. My head and vision pulsated in thick, nauseating waves. I threw up again, this time making it into the toilet bowl. What came out of me was red.

*Am I bleeding?*

Urgently, I clung to the toilet to get a closer look, but it was hard to focus. Everything was spinning as if I were on a merry-go-round in The Twilight Zone. I didn't remember eating anything with red coloring in it, but I had heard *aragy* was sometimes made with gasoline. I'd also heard a bad batch could cause a person to go blind. And here I was drinking it, *willingly*. I was the quintessential rat in the cage addicted and unable to stop pressing the lever even though it was melting the flesh off my hand right before my very eyes.

"Help me," I choked. "Please...somebody, help me!" But nobody was there.

I needed water immediately. It took considerable effort to pull myself up to the sink, but once I did I splashed it all over my face. I was burning up inside. Frantically, I doused my face again and in the process, I caught sight of my reflection in the mirror. My skin was a sickly yellowish color and my eyes were inflamed and pink. My pores, massive holes. I was the spitting image of a real-life monster.

"I hate you!" I cursed at my reflection. My foul face cursed back. I hit the glass with the palm of my hand. The revenge hurt.

I leaned down and puked again all over the floor. Losing my balance in the muck, I fell to the ground with a thud. Above me, the fan whirled around and around.

*Luke will find my body. My parents will never see me alive again. This is it.*

I blacked out.

***

Like a fall leaf sinking in a gutter, I woke up wrecked. A rancid smell stung my nostrils. My eyes popped open. I tried to move, but the left side of my body was bruised and achy and my throat throbbed.

*Where am I?*

Blinking through a web of soggy hair, I recognized the fan above me. It whirred as if nothing had happened. Memories from the previous night burst through my skull all at once: the *aragy*, the gasoline, the fear of dying.

*Please, no.*

Lying on my side, I brought my knees to my chest and wrapped my arms around them while squeezing my eyes together tightly. I tried to shut out the truth I couldn't bear to face:

*I'll always be a stupid, obnoxious drunk no matter how hard I try.*

The shame fed on my soul until it was shriveled up and all that remained was a miserable, distant ache. Next it devoured my hope and all the progress I'd made, and then it sucked up the last particle of light, which I'd been safe-keeping in my heart *just in case...*

Consumed by addiction's black hole, I lost myself to the darkness.

\*\*\*

My insides burned for days, and I fretted over whether or not to see a doctor. But Sudanese hospitals weren't known for sanitation or quality healthcare, so I never went. Eventually my body repaired itself, and after a week I felt somewhat normal. My real or imagined brush with death—while terrifying—had helped me realize something completely unexpected.

I'd done some really good work in Sudan.

I couldn't give up now and risk losing it all. I wanted to give this recovery thing another try.

But pulling myself out of that black hopeless hell was like trying to walk with two hundred tons of cement strapped to my ankles and a monkey on my back. This monkey wasn't the same one that most people claimed was on their backs. Mine had fangs, beady piss-colored eyes, and sharp knives jutting from its head. I called him my Shame Monkey because he was there to remind me of my awful relapse.

"You're a devil!" he barked. (He could talk.) "You can't be trusted and must rot in hell!"

I took a sledgehammer and whacked him whenever I could, but I was a lousy shot.

To overcome my shame, I'd need to be more strategic. I didn't want to be stuck between relapse and recovery for the rest of my life. I'd been completely blindsided by my overwhelming urge to drink and by the fact that I'd so easily given in to that urge. As I searched through my journal for clues as to how it had happened, I came across an old entry, which I'd written right after Garang's death. There it was, a note to self:

*The next time you relapse—which I doubt you will because you're doing so awesome!—try being kind and loving to yourself like you were with the Sudanese today. And they killed people, Shan. If you can find compassion for them, you should be able to give it to yourself too. Focus on the positive and how far you've come. It will make it easier for you to get back up. Don't you forget this. (I have a feeling you will.)*

The tables had turned. This time I was the one who, under extreme stress, had fallen back on old coping patterns. During the riots I'd been open to the Sudanese and their struggles, and even considered their behaviors without judgment. Could I do the same for myself? I had certainly been under a great deal of stress and I knew in my heart I hadn't meant to harm anybody.

I decided I could try and be compassionate, but first I needed to develop a Relapse Prevention Plan of Action in case instability flared up in Khartoum. (It wouldn't be the first time, that's for sure.) My plan included healthy ways of handling stress that didn't involve alcohol. Since lack of sleep had played a huge role in my mental downward spiral, I wrote that I could purchase a natural sleeping aid at the local *suk*. I also wrote that I could seek out new ways to experience Sudan that would bring more balance to my mind, body, and soul. After so many hours of fieldwork, I knew that Khartoum was a treasure trove of organizations dedicated to making a difference. Why not volunteer for a few of them?

On paper, everything looked solid. If only my shame monkey would get a clue. No matter how many times I whacked him good, he just kept bouncing back. I was tired of the game. Fighting wasn't as interesting as it had been when I was a kid. As an adult, I understood what my dad had meant when he'd said: *I want peace, not justice.* So, one day, I put the sledgehammer down, and just as the monkey went to tackle me, I turned to face him.

"What do you want? And why can't we just talk it out? Everything is always so dramatic and hurtful with you. It's not very effective in creating change, you know?"

"You're a devil! You can't be trusted and must rot in hell!" he shouted.

I rolled my eyes, "You need new material like you need a new strategy. This is just getting old."

It dawned on me that I'd heard these words before. They were the exact words that my childhood monsters accused me of for not being interested in the Mormon Church. While living in Sudan I'd begun to make sense of that situation and even establish peace with how I was treated for seeking out my own path. I saw that if I'd grown up in Khartoum I probably would've been Muslim. And I probably would've found a way to break free of Islam too, *and* I probably would've been ostracized and humiliated for wanting to do so.

This didn't mean I was a bad person. It meant that people and whole communities will often try to use force and fear to get their way with you, and that despite the enormous pressure to conform, I had been brave enough to listen to and pursue my inner truth—the truth that worked best for *me* and *my* goals and *my* perceptions and *my* personality.

Shame is a result of comparing yourself to other people's expectations of you. It's not an accurate reflection of behavior or a person's soul or value. The shame I was experiencing as a result of my relapse was exactly that, a reflection of harmful comparisons and expectations that I'd internalized over the years. It wasn't related to the fact that I had a drink or got drunk—and understanding this was key. If I could learn to handle myself with a little more care and flexibility, I could get through this. In time, I could even bring the shame associated with my addiction into the light and use logic and rationality to help it heal just like I was learning to do with the shame associated with my spiritual choices.

Seriously, who wants to chase around an imaginary monkey for the rest of their life with an imaginary sledgehammer?

\*\*\*

I kept busy with IRIN and school. For IRIN, I switched my focus to writing hot news stories so I could get quotes over the phone from agency leads, so I could avoid going into the field and exposing myself to sad stories as much as possible. I needed a break from the harsh reality around me. This was another part of my Relapse Prevention Plan of Action.

Yet I still longed to write creatively.

I had heard of *Al Bab (The Door)* magazine, a definitive guide to living and working in Sudan. The magazine had been founded by an Irish man named John who believed that the media focus on Sudan was too negative. *Al Bab* provided the opportunity to focus on the positive things that were happening around Sudan, and specifically it celebrated Sudanese culture, programs, and communities, which was pretty unusual for a country so ravaged by war.

I emailed John to tell him I adored what the magazine stood for and wanted to be a part of it. I attached my resume and writing samples and pitched a few ideas that might bring some fun energy to his magazine. One idea belonged to Kate, a vivacious woman working as the Public Information Officer for the American Embassy. Kate and I ate out once a week and had gotten into the habit of discussing the food, service, menu options, ambiance, and location. Kate had the idea that I should write restaurant reviews for *Al Bab* so people knew what their options were.

Another idea I threw at John in an attempt to connect the people of Sudan to one another in a more personal and upbeat way was to create a piece called "On the Street," which would consist of asking random people a variety of questions: what's your favorite thing about Sudan? What's the funniest thing that's happened to you while living here? Who's your daddy? Okay, not that last question—but that's the point. The questions were meant to put a smile on the face of the readers. Next to each person's response I wanted to put their picture so that their responses were more tangible. I also suggested writing a travel diary because there were a few places I still wanted to see, including Suakin Island, a deserted port in the Red Sea that was once a great coral city and crucial to powerful empires. The city still stands, but it's now a crumbling relic of coral embedded with polished and shimmering seashells. I hoped with my travel logs to inspire people to get out and explore.

John called right away. He wanted to hire me on a freelance basis but was concerned about money. "Right now, we're struggling financially. I guess not too many people are interested in reading a magazine with strictly positive content. Go figure!"

That was John. He was a feisty young man who was as charming as he was rambunctious, but he knew what he was up against when he started this endeavor, and he wasn't one to give up so easily. "We could really use you and your ideas to bring some fresh energy to the magazine and help us turn this thing around."

I told him I was willing to work for free, no strings attached. It was the least I could do for a place and community that was helping me find myself.

***

One of my favorite discoveries was a farm in Bahri owned by a British woman named Jane-anne Khalid. At the farm, Jane-anne ran a program called Miracles: Sudan Hippotherapy. ("Hippo" is the Greek word for horse). The goal of the program was to help disabled children normalize muscle tone and equilibrium reactions, head and trunk controls, and coordination through the use of horses. Many of the children seeking services at her farm were orphans and had been diagnosed with cerebral palsy, a common disability in Sudan due to lack of healthcare systems and facilities, and untreated bouts of malaria and meningitis. The hippotherapy classes were free for orphans, who showed up to the farm in droves for the opportunity to "ride high" as Jane-anne liked to put it. She believed the horses helped build their confidence, too.

Jane-anne and I had met a few months ago while I was researching resource gaps for individuals living with disabilities and I'd fallen in love with her and her farm instantly. I had promised to one day return and be at her beck and call, whatever she needed.

Now, here I was.

"Shan, these children have very little space in the world where they're loved and accepted. Most of the time they're not even allowed to go to school, and their parents keep them hidden inside because there's such a stigma against them. The farm provides a place for them to exist and be joyful."

We'd been walking in circles around the farm for nearly an hour while taking turns with a few of the orphans that had come for their hippotherapy session. I was seated on the back of a sandy brown horse with shimmery highlights and white spots on her rear. In between my legs sat Hanady, a little girl in braids and tattered jeans. During our sessions, I'd sit on the horse's back to hold the children in place while Jane-anne walked beside us and held onto the reigns so we didn't fly off. Typically when the kids started off their bodies were stiff, but after a few loops they eased into the ride and went with the flow.

"It gives the parents a place to interact, too. Initially, they're really reluctant to talk to anyone because they've been in isolation. But after a while they feel welcome and make friends," Jane-anne said with a shrug.

During these sessions, Jane-anne would go on and on about anything and everything. She would ramble for hours if I let her, which meant I rarely got a word in—but I was happy. The farm became my refuge like the field I used to kick back and relax in as a kid. I think the sun had an affinity for it, too, because it would set over her emerald green gardens in the prettiest pink, gold, and orange hues I'd ever seen. As Jane-anne continued to talk, we looped the farm and I'd fall into a soothing rhythm as if I were a child again rocking in my mother's arms.

"Good God! If you only knew how much it has cost me to keep these horses alive. Next thing you know, they'll need my arms and legs. When I came to Sudan years ago my plan was to save one maltreated horse, maybe two. Now it's what, thirty years later? And look where we are."

When she spoke it was with great passion and intensity. In her previous life I imagined she was a famous actress on Broadway.

I went to say something, but stopped. She wasn't done.

"Money," Jane-anne started again. "It's too bad everything comes down to this because if it didn't, you know what I could do? I could afford food for all of Sudan's starving horses, and then we could train them to provide therapy for all our orphans. Wouldn't that be the cat's meow?"

I stifled a giggle and nodded. "Yes, it absolutely would."

After our final loop for the day, Jane-anne helped Hanady off her horse, and the two of us walked over to a spot in the shade near a turquoise Volkswagen beetle that hadn't moved since I'd first discovered the farm. We plopped down on a pile of dust and a handful of overexcited puppies ran over to welcome us. Covered in clumps of dirt and who-knows-what-else, they jumped into our laps, but neither of us minded.

"There was one time when seven of my horses all fell ill at once. I'd put so much of my time and money into saving them, so I wasn't about to let them go without a fight. I worked night and day to ensure they were cared for, but a storm came and soaked the ground, making it hard for them to recover. My husband kept saying, 'You can't save the world by saving these seven horses. You have to come in from the storm or you'll fall ill too,'" she said as she wrapped two puppies in her arms and held them close.

"But I had no other choice. They'd become my family. Sarah, she was my favorite, so when she fell ill it crushed me. I'd found her in the desert years back. She was alone, starving, nearly dead. But she had moxie. When we made eye contact, I knew she was worth investing in." She paused and gazed into the cotton candy sunset.

"She *was* worth it. She left me a mare just before she died and today she's just like her mama: spunky, hardworking, fun. We call her Ally and she was the only horse to survive through all of that."

Jane-anne looked at the ground suddenly and I sensed she needed a moment to herself, so I turned my back and began to play with the puppies, who were eager for my attention. While two tugged at my pant legs, one jumped up to lick my chin. His attitude reminded me of Fred.

I read somewhere that pets are our spiritual companions, and in some other dimension they make a pact with us to provide the thing we need most in order to help us through critical life moments. Perhaps it sounds silly, but Fred came into my life when I was devastatingly isolated, working around the clock, and my loneliness was like heavy clothing. He was a comedian at heart. If only you could see him jumping in and out of the shower like I do in my mind's eye, you would understand that he really got a kick out of making me laugh.

I was pretty sure he'd forgiven me for what I'd done to him. One day, I hoped I could forgive me, too—for everything.

\*\*\*

Two months later, I was still sober and my life was rich with meaningful projects for IRIN, *Al Bab*, the farm, and Unity High. *Alhamdullilah*. I'd caught the service bug pretty bad and decided I wanted to volunteer at a center in Khartoum that had been established by a local Christian church to provide guidance, board, and education to fifty young Sudanese orphans.

I had heard about the center from Linda, a teacher at Unity, and asked what I could do to be of service. She told me that the kids were in need of some extracurricular activities, so we decided I would teach art classes once per week. But first Linda thought I should come to the center to meet everyone.

Upon my arrival I was greeted by a teenage boy who smelled and looked like he hadn't bathed in years. As I walked past him and into the compound, he feasted his eyes on my body as though I were a hooker in Amsterdam's Red Light District. In the corner of my eye, I could see more boys standing in a corner next to a watering hole. They whistled at me as I looked around nervously for Linda, who popped out of a dark doorway a few moments later.

"Glad you could make it." She was a small, timid woman with graying hair and crooked, stained teeth.

"Sure," I said, feeling awkward and exposed as the boys gawked at me. "Where are all the girls?" I asked quietly.

"Girls?" Linda asked, put out by my question. She lowered her voice. "This is an all-boys home." Linda explained that, in fact, this was a home for Sudan's Lost Boys.

I knew all about the Lost Boys of Sudan. When the civil war broke out, they'd fled their homes and families in the south in fear of being killed or forced to fight in violent armies. There were about 20,000 Lost Boys total. Most were young boys — six or seven years old — when they fled by foot to Ethiopia, a thousand-mile journey. Over half of them died before they got there. The other half wandered for years in and out of Africa's war zones suffering from hunger, dehydration, and exhaustion. Some were killed by wild animals while others drowned crossing rivers. Many others were caught and killed in combat. In 1991, war broke out in Ethiopia and sent the young refugees fleeing once again. Eventually, they found refuge in Kenya. In 2001, thousands of Lost Boys would resettle throughout the United States, including in Salt Lake City, Utah.

"*Lackma!*" one boy yelled in my direction. *Meat.*

I swallowed hard and tried to hide my disappointment. My experience with the Lost Boys usually went like this. They were disrespectful and crude. Worse, they were violent. I'd seen them throw bricks and rocks at an innocent bystander once or twice, and as a result they made me extremely uneasy.

"I hate to do this, but I—" I whispered. "I think it's best if I work with girls. Is there another center I can volunteer at?"

Linda frowned. "That's too bad. They've been looking forward to this all week."

"I'm sorry, I just don't think I can be very effective here," I said. The boys were still whistling and catcalling.

Linda glared at them and they stopped. "I understand, but the Lost Boys are the most neglected of all the populations in Sudan. God knows they're not the easiest to get along with—" she shrugged. "Can't you stay for group and then decide?"

I agreed to at least do that, and as she began to show me around the grimy, circular compound, an older southern boy walked over. He was probably seventeen and his eyes and teeth glowed like snow in the moonlight. His name was Abraham.

"Welcome," he greeted and we shook hands. "We are very excited to have you here Miss Shannon. Linda has told me a great deal about you and the work you do for our country." He gestured at the boys. "Please do not be alarmed by them. It is all for show, they mean no harm." Then he ran off and gathered up the boys into a room out of view.

Once he was out of earshot, Linda said, "Abraham was enslaved during the war. Soldiers broke into his village, killed all the adults, and took the children to work for them. The girls were forced to work as sex slaves while the boys did hard labor. When Abraham escaped the first time, the solders found him, and in order to make an example out of him, they stabbed him in the waist with a knife, and nailed his feet to a board. He still has the scars."

"He's a diabetic," she continued. "And he's had a hard time regulating himself. The other day he went to the market to buy new clothes and on his way back he collapsed in an *umjot*. The driver pushed him out of the car and into a ditch, and a policeman, assuming that he was drunk, threw him in jail. The experience really hurt him; he's a sensitive kid."

She walked me over to the room where the boys sat. There were about fifteen of them in a circle. I smiled bashfully as I sat down next to a boy who was probably about six. Linda sat on my left. Once everyone was settled, a scrawny boy who was probably about ten years old stood. Linda leaned over to tell me his name was Ahmed.

"I know we are all trying to stay sober," Ahmed spoke to his peers in Arabic; my heart skipped. "But I am having a really hard time giving it up and I want to ask you, my friends, if you will please pray for me."

Crammed in between Linda and the six year old, I was suddenly claustrophobic. Beads of perspiration oozed from my pores. *Where is the fan or AC or even a cracked window when you need one?* I wondered. I was worried that Ahmed's dirty little secret and his very public confession would somehow expose my own. Could Linda sense my shame? She had to. It was now radiating from every atom in every cell of my body like electromagnetic radiation. Guilt-ridden, I shifted my weight from side to side.

Linda leaned over to me and shamefaced, I flushed. *Busted*.

Whispering in my ear, she explained that the boys had caught Ahmed sneaking glue into the facility and they wanted both him and the substance removed right away. He'd been given too many chances, and the boys were worried about their own recovery, so they'd concluded it was best for everyone at the center if Ahmed left.

"Please don't throw me on the streets. If you do, I'll die," Ahmed pleaded. He was focused on his hands, fiddling his fingers. It was hard to imagine living his life. What would it be like to grow up in a war without the support and love of a parent? Even though my parents and I had certainly had our moments, their support, love, and guidance would play a critical role in my recovery. In fact, I wouldn't have been able to do it without them. Glue was probably one of the only ways for the boys to escape from their traumas.

On average, over 50% of the world's refugees and IDPs are torture survivors. In addition to devastating physical injury, these survivors of torture and severe war trauma have a high prevalence of complex and co-existing mental health issues such as PTSD, severe forms of anxiety and depression, and psychosis.

"Why don't we pray together right now?" Abraham suggested. He stood up. It was clear to me that he was the leader of the group and that the boys looked up to him. One by one, our circle began to stand. The little boy seated next to me reached out to take my hand. He looked up at me with curious eyes, and then closed his. I reached for Linda's and we prayed.

"Dear Heavenly Father," Abraham began. "Help Ahmed, help us all that we may feel our importance in this world and our self-worth. Help us so we can be great leaders for our country as we grow into men, and help us with our addiction that we may be able to stay strong and not give in to temptation."

I could hardly believe it. In the middle of Khartoum, among the Lost Boys of Sudan, I'd stumbled into a makeshift twelve-step meeting, and this was their version of the Unity Prayer. I opened my eyes and looked around. Instead of bowing their heads, many of the boys had their faces pointed up toward the ceiling with their eyes open. They were staring in thoughtful concentration as though their dedicated focus could wash away their sins and the fact that they were abandoned and addicted.

After group was over, I promised Linda I'd return the next week with some art supplies, and then Abraham walked me to the gate.

"Hey, that was cool by the way, what you did for Ahmed." I held my hand up to high five him.

"He's my brother. He would have done the same for me," he said, high fiving me back.

I hesitated. I'd been debating over whether or not to share my dirty little secret with him. "Abraham, I—I have two months."

He stared at me blankly. "Miss?" He blinked.

"Sober. I have two months sober."

"You, miss? No!" He shook his head in disbelief.

"I do! I mean, not glue or anything, but alcohol. You know *aragy*?" I put my hand up to my mouth and made the shape of a bottle.

Abraham shook his head again, "I can't believe it."

"I've had some slip-ups, but I haven't had one drop for two whole months now. I'm pretty proud. What about you?"

"I have one month, miss. I've had some slip-ups, too." He looked down at the ground and began to push around a small rock with his shoe. I thought of the scars on his feet, but I couldn't see any because he was wearing sneakers. Perhaps his relapse was the reason he'd been so compassionate with Ahmed.

"Will you tell the others for me?"

He shook his head, "Are you sure? I'm not sure you should share something like this...as a woman."

"Yes, I'm sure. I want them to know."

Abraham nodded and shook my hand. *"Ashuuf kum Insha'Allah saldig." See you again if God wills it, my friend.*

At this point in my life, I'd only told a handful of people about my addiction because I couldn't bear the thought of being judged for it. Although I knew my behavior was a *symptom of emotional and mental suffering,* so many others viewed it as a *moral failing.* That made it really difficult to open up and ask for help.

But it has been said that silence is deadly; if we hide with our secrets in the shadows, they will eventually kill us. Knowing that I could share my struggles with Abraham and the boys without being judged—because they'd been there and would understand—helped me feel less alone in my messy, imperfect quest for recovery.

Today, I share about my addiction and recovery journey as often as possible because I don't want to die all alone in a dark closet, shrouded in shame beside the decomposing skeletons I tried so desperately to hide.

I want to live.

# Chapter 12

"*A*re you sure you want to go home now? Your career is booming, girl!" said Kate from the American Embassy as she bit down on a fried potato.

It was lunchtime and we were at the Coral Khartoum Hotel situated at the junction of the Blue and White Nile Rivers, enjoying an all-you-can-eat-buffet like stereotypical Americans. I nodded as I chewed on a piece of *tamia* and washed it down with a swig of *karkadé,* a rosy-red hibiscus tea traditionally toasted at Sudanese wedding celebrations and said to have been a preferred drink of the pharaohs.

Kate was right. My career *was* booming. Months earlier, at the Friendship Hall (the largest International Conference Hall in Sudan), I'd hit a career high when IRIN asked me to attend the African Union (AU) Summit. For Africa and politics, it doesn't get much bigger than the AU Summit, and over thirty African Presidents and other renowned world leaders and journalists had flown in to see who would be elected for the 2006 AU Chairmanship, a highly sought-after one-year position elected by the Assembly of Heads of State.

This year, Bashir was up for the post, which of course caused major drama since he was still being investigated by the ICC for human rights violations in Darfur. Fortunately, the President of the Republic of Congo, Denis Sassou Nguesso, was given the honor instead. Bashir was promised a shot at the chairmanship in 2007 but due to the increased tension in Darfur, Ghanaian President, John Kufuor, was elected instead. (The government of Chad had threatened to withdraw its membership if Sudan assumed the chair). Overall, covering the event had been quite a rush; I'd had to pinch myself several times to make sure it was really happening.

Things were going well with *Al Bab,* too. I was contributing about 25 percent of the content and pictures for John's magazine, and both my restaurant reviews and *On the Street* section had been well received. The responses I got from strangers and friends regarding their favorite things about Sudan had been interesting:

"One of my favorite things about Sudan is Tuti Island! I love wondering around the lush vegetation as the sun sets and spotting lizards and butterflies while feeling like you are in a another world, away from the hustle-bustle of everyday life in Khartoum," said my neighbor Martha Hemsted from the United Kingdom.

"My favorite place is the bowling alley at Afra Mall. It's nice to go have a game with friends and go out for a meal after a hard day's work," said Alan Tin-Win from Yangon Myanmar, a teacher friend from Unity.

"I enjoy the beaches on the river Nile. They're comforting—a great place to sit and reflect," said Murad from southern Sudan.

One of the photos from my adventures at Suakin Island, the abandoned coral island by the Red Sea, was chosen for the magazine's latest cover, which also happened to be *Al Bab's* one-year anniversary edition, and John had recently asked me to work for him as an assistant editor in order to help spread the magazine to Juba and Kenya. I was also running an aerobics class called High Energy at Tea and Things, a chic women's club where Sudan's most respected expat and local ladies came to break a sweat and read girly magazines. On top of this, I'd had a well-read feature on Sudan's HIV and AIDS epidemic published in the *Forced Migration Review*. (This was co-written by Derk Segaar, a talented writer, photographer, and UN staff member.) It would be an understatement to say I'd come a long way. The world was at my fingertips. If only it felt as good as it sounded, I'd be golden.

"I'm tired, Kate. Burned out. All I can think of is a nice bath and *real* air conditioning," I exhaled slowly, stabbing at the *tamia* and salad on my plate. For months I'd been troubled over whether or not to stay in Khartoum or go back home to Utah, and both options were highly distressing.

"You can always rent a room here for the night," Kate suggested.

I wanted to point out that the water in this hotel was probably a creamy beige like it had been at the high-class hotel in Kenya I'd stayed in during IRIN's media training, but even if the water were clear at the Coral, it didn't matter. I was still in Khartoum, and quite frankly, I was Rhett Butler (from *Gone with the Wind*) and *I just didn't give a damn*—about any of it.

"It's not the same," was all I said, and wiped my mouth with my sleeve.

"Are you okay, Shan? You seem…down."

I shrugged and took another gulp of *karkadé* in order to clean out the bits of fried chick peas crowding out my teeth. Kate, old enough to be my grandmother, had that tender, maternal intuition. But that didn't mean I wanted to talk about it. As a career-oriented person, I knew that leaving Sudan at this particular time was a bad idea, especially considering how hard I'd worked to get here. I was in a prime position to take it to the next level. IRIN had asked me to go to Somalia to cover some stories there, and if I stayed I'd get to go to Juba, the south of Sudan, like I'd always wanted, to cover peacebuilding and renovations happening there now that the war was over. If I played my cards right, in just a few short years, I could be the next Farah.

Yet when all was said and done, I wasn't well physically, mentally, or spiritually, and hadn't been since visiting Darfur nearly five months before. I'd emerged from there as a creature from *The Walking Dead*, my pulse flat-lined and in desperate need of resuscitation. Although the AU Summit had been exciting—I was covering world news from a room filled with some of the most powerful and most-wanted people on our planet!—I felt more disconnected than ever. I wanted to be excited and grateful for all the opportunities that were flowing my way, and I wanted to feel the passion I felt for travel and exploration like I did when I'd first gotten here, but every time I tried to expand my butterfly wings and jump into the moment with any gusto, I fell to the ground with an unglamorous thud.

I'd even canceled a trip to Israel where I was supposed to meet my parents and my brother, Ryan, in just a few short weeks. I had bought the three of them plane tickets with some of my hard-earned money because I wanted them to have the thrill of exploring the world, too. For my parents, visiting the place of Christ's resurrection was a lifelong dream, and I was happy I had the means to make it come true. But the thought of being overstimulated by a new culture felt more taxing than anything. I'd seen enough, and all I wanted to do was stand still at the top of the Wasatch Mountains in the cool, crisp air and figure out what it all meant.

"I'm okay, thanks, Kate. Do you want dessert?" I got up from the table, walked over to the buffet, and stared vacantly at the rows of tasty Sudanese sweets.

All of my favorites were there: *basta*, a simple dessert with a strong peanut flavor, *basboosa*, a semolina-based cake soaked in lemon syrup, and my absolute favorite, *baseema,* a batter-based cake with a hint of coconut.

Kate walked over and put her hand on my shoulder. "That baklava looks divine!" she said, peering over me. She swooped in and grabbed a slice teeming with sliced nuts.

I moped. I wasn't in the mood for anything Sudanese. Luckily there was a *normal*-looking slice of fluffy, white cake that had a cute frosted bow on top. I snatched it up, sat down, and stabbed at the slice contemplatively with my fork.

"Didn't you already tell your family you were staying for another year? What'd they say?"

A small smile crept over my face at the memory of the phone conversation I'd had with my sister, Holly, a couple of weeks back. When I'd broken the news to her that I was thinking of staying another year, she'd actually shouted at me:

"Shannon, this is ridiculous! You can't live in Africa for the rest of your life. You belong *here* with your *family*. What about the kids? Have you thought about them? They shouldn't have to grow up without their aunt. It's not right."

Holly's passionate response was her typical way of expressing her vulnerability without having to blatantly articulate it. It was one her most endearing traits. I knew that beneath her angry outburst, she missed me. I missed her, too.

"They weren't too happy about it," I said, thinking of the kids and how much they'd grown since I'd seen them. I missed our Sunday family walks to the canal to see the neighborhood ducks. I missed over-the-top Target commercials at Christmastime and having nothing to worry about but whether I should finish college or not. I missed being able to walk outside in a tank top and shorts without being cursed by black magic. I missed blending in with the crowd and not being a minority.

"What if you went back to visit for a couple of months to get some R&R? Then you can come back out?"

Kate saw me as a younger version of herself. She was unmarried and had dedicated her life to world travel and humanitarian work. She thought I belonged out in the wild, a solo woman traveling free—and so did I. I just hadn't factored in the effects of long-term exposure to poverty, war, and disease. If I left I risked giving up my big dreams, but I was also worried about my sobriety. In America I'd get to blend in—which was great—but this meant I'd have to start from scratch with my career, and that meant working at some lame call center that would certainly suck the soul right out of me. I was worried about fitting in with my Mormon community, too. It had been tough enough as a struggling alcoholic who didn't want to marry or go to church. How would I relate to anybody now? Who would I talk to about this experience that would even care or understand?

"Maybe," I let the sentence hang, poked at the cake bow, and then smashed it with my fork. While my sister was certain I belonged in Utah next to her and our family, and Kate was certain I belonged out in the wild, I wasn't so sure where I belonged anymore.

Kate watched me closely. "Well, school is out in just two weeks, my dear. You'll have to decide pretty soon, won't you?"

I stared indifferently at a busboy cleaning a table. Deep down, I knew that staying was no longer an option. I needed time for self-care. I didn't know what that looked like—only that I couldn't do it here.

"I think I've made up my mind."

It was done. The spirit of Artemis, that Greek Goddess of the Wilderness and the Hunt who'd struck me with an arrow in the first place, had left me. Now I was Dorothy from the Wizard of Oz, and all I wanted to do was tap together a pair of sparkly, red heels and get the hell out of Khartoum.

\*\*\*

Once I'd made the decision to leave Khartoum, all of the fears and frustrations I'd been bottling up since day one rose to the surface like a sci-fi creature off the coast of Singapore waving a dozen tentacles and looking like a nightmare. Unbeknown to me, a big part of me had been white-knuckling it this entire time, not only while in Darfur. The solo adventure meant to test my survival turned out to be way more than I'd bargained for. I'd witnessed a historic peace deal, had an Uzi whipped out in class, watched AIDS-affected individuals proudly proclaim their status in one of the largest slums in the world, endured a coup, mourned the death of a war hero, and underwent countless hours of strenuous fieldwork. And then there was the genocide. I could hardly believe all I'd seen and done, and I was just now admitting to myself how incredibly hard it had all been. As overwhelming emotions broke to the surface of my conscious mind, I became consumed with panic. Sudan's robust desert was now fast-moving quicksand, and sinking in it, I was desperate to get out.

But it wasn't over yet. Sudan had one last fiery hoop for me to jump through.

According to the Ministry of Humanitarian Affairs, the BES tax situation had never been resolved, and I still owed money: $3,500. I wasn't prepared to spend my last days debating with the tax people. I had so many loose ends to tie up, but it was hard to focus on them because another deep-seated fear had reared its ugly head: that I'd get stuck in Sudan *forever*. I'd heard stories of travelers getting arrested for petty crimes in foreign countries and then being imprisoned for years. Secretly, I thought this *would* happen to me. If my work visa ran out, and if they didn't grant me an exit visa, I'd be in the country illegally, which meant the Sudanese government had a right to throw me in jail.

For several days in a row I went to the tax department to try and sort things out. Roby, a man with the kindest, saddest eyes I'd ever seen, was assigned to my case. Each day I explained my story to him he responded with:

"*Bookra, Insha'Allah.*" *Tomorrow, God willing.*

Every time he said this, my panic increased. I was running out of time. Under the stress, my panic attacks returned more intensely than ever. On the fourth consecutive day, I was on the verge of a full-on breakdown. I only had one week to get out legally.

As I approached Roby that morning, he smiled at me, his mouth full of decaying teeth. He offered me some *shai,* which I usually accepted but declined that morning because my stomach burned like it was chock-full of acid. Wearily, I asked Roby if he'd heard anything from BES and if they'd paid up.

"*Bookra, insha'Allah,*" he said gently. I didn't want to break, but it was too late.

"No!" I screamed suddenly and slammed my fist down on the table. Roby's tea cup rattled. "Screw you and your stupid *insha'Allah!*"

I recoiled, horrified by my outburst. Roby's sensitive eyes widened. I looked around the room to find everyone staring at me. I'd worked so hard to make space for my Muslim friends and their beliefs, and now I had deeply offended this man, Roby, who had done absolutely nothing wrong. He was just doing his job. As my despair hit a new low, I searched for a way to apologize, but my mind was flooded with trepidation and I couldn't think straight. I worried over what might actually come out of my mouth if I opened it again, and I didn't know how to explain to Roby that I was falling apart because of all the suffering I'd seen over the past two years—when this was his *everyday life.*

Reaching over, Roby patted my hand tenderly, "*Shwaya, shwaya, saldig.*"

I pulled back as if he'd attacked me with a dentist's drill. Didn't he know this phrase was the last thing on earth I wanted to hear? It was worse than listening to an opera made up of a dozen acrylic nails and a chalkboard. I gasped for air. Today was not the day I was going to lose it completely. I'd be turning twenty-seven soon, which meant I was nearly two years older and wiser than when I'd first come. I'd withstood a lot worse. I could relax. I could keep my cool.

I walked back to my chair and stood facing the wall. Hot tears welled in the corner of my eyes. My throat and chest constricted as the office walls narrowed in. Placing my hand on the wall, I leaned my head against it and closed my eyes, trying to block everything out.

*Breathe.*

A few moments of strangulated breathing passed by. Then I felt a tap on my shoulder. It was Roby. He said that my debt had been forgiven, and in his hand was the permission slip I needed to go home.

The kindness of the Sudanese never ceased to amaze me, especially considering all they'd been through. I realized that beneath my anger and frustration was a cesspool of grief and sorrow I didn't know what to do with. I'd fallen deeply for these people and their traditions.

How would I ever say goodbye?

I wasn't just some random person that had passed through while on vacation. I had *lived* a *life* here. I had worked intimately alongside them—as their friend—celebrating their milestones while seeking understanding for their setbacks. And I would never see them again—at least not in this capacity. Sudan is not some tropical getaway destination. You can't just grab a tourist visa and hop on over. No, tourists weren't allowed in this war-torn country, which meant I would never argue again with a cab driver over how many dinars I owed him. I would never wake up with the *adhan* blasting out my eardrums or sit on a mat and eat *ful* and *tamia* with the locals. I was losing an entire race and culture all at once, and the loss felt astronomical.

*"Shukran jizelan,"* I said shaking Roby's hand.

His face lit up at the sight of my relief. We were two unlikely friends from two vastly different worlds and for a brief moment in time, we'd come together like a stellular collision, and through the force of gravity we had merged into one vibrant entity.

When stars collide—depending on how fast they're moving— the collision can be tremendously violent, or, if they're moving at slower velocities, it can be a gentle, even happy mixing of two great lights. In my freaked out and manic state, I worried Roby and I had collided head-on. When stars collide in this manner they splash one another's guts to the far corners of the galaxy. Perhaps I'd collided head-on with the Sudanese in more circumstances than I was willing to admit to. Perhaps I'd been less humble than I originally thought.

But in Sudan, a super large country with uniquely explosive energy and violence, it seemed head-on collisions were an everyday occurrence, the main way of connecting to another. In this way, Sudan was like a supermassive black hole made up of millions of solar masses buried at the heart of a distant galaxy. A supermassive black hole has one of the most vaporous, magnetic, and violent atmospheres around. One may form from a high-energy collision and is defined by exhibiting such a strong gravitational pull that no particle can escape from it. Yet when matter falls onto a black hole it can form an accretion disk heated by friction creating some of the brightest objects in the universe.

As I felt Roby's hand in mine, *knowing* surged through me. I knew that I was blessed to have orbited over to his cataclysmic world where the ferocious smashing of guts were a given: I was also blessed to escape it. I knew that the chaos in our interaction was less important than the fact that we had, for whatever reason, vibrated into one another's sphere of being.

Roby and I had fused, amalgamated, melded, mixed, intermingled; we had *made a connection*.

Although our interaction was messy and brief, it didn't take away from the possible truth rooted in all human contact: there was a great purpose in it, and despite the fact that the rippling effects were invisible in that moment, Roby and I had expanded because of it.

*** 

Once I had my exit visa, I contacted John and Erich to let them know I was headed home, and although they were disappointed, they understood. School had ended weeks earlier and I'd already bid my lovely Unity students *adieu*. I went to Bahri to say goodbye to Jane-anne, the horses, and the orphans. But I'd avoided saying goodbye to almost everyone else in person, including my BES students, even though I really wanted to invite them to Afra's outdoor playground for one last hurrah. I didn't go see William at the *Khartoum Monitor* or Bushra, my translator with IRIN. I was starting to realize that my "Darfur mantra" was a longtime motto of mine. When things got tough, I ran away like a scared little girl. I hoped to one day break these patterns but right then I didn't know how.

If there was one group of individuals I *had* to see before I left, it was Abraham and the Lost Boys. We'd been painting a mural on a wall at the center, and I swore to them we'd complete it as a team. The project had taken longer than expected due to a nasty *haboob* that had been followed by an unexpected rainstorm. This had destroyed our hard work, but not our convictions. I bought stronger paint and we started over. The boys had taken this whole art thing very seriously and had been good sports throughout the entire process.

Ever since I'd told Abraham about my addiction, the boys had treated me differently. I don't know what was said exactly, but they never cat-called again. I sensed they still had their guards up, which was okay—they'd been through a lot—but they handled me as if I were fragile. Our common suffering had bonded us.

The language barrier made it difficult for us to have heartfelt conversations about our struggles, so mostly we'd paint side by side, occasionally making eye contact and smiling shyly at one another. This was our routine. We also danced. The boys had an old boom box and a tape of Nelly's *Sweatsuit* album. We played it over and over again shaking our tail feathers as we worked.

On my last day, we began our art project as Nelly sang for us to "drop down and get our eagles on." While I focused on applying bright hues in strategic places, the boys bobbed up and down looking cool. I'd named the mural Pictures of Promise and asked each boy to paint something that would inspire them to believe in their worth and purpose whenever they looked at it. Some had painted pictures of Christ or the future families they wished for. One boy painted a picture of himself as a doctor. My picture was an outline of Sudan and in it I sketched an array of dynamic characters encompassed in swirls of apricot-colored dust.

When we first started painting, Ahmed had asked, "Why Sudan, miss?"

"Because the Sudanese showed me kindness and compassion," I said. "Living here has helped me discover that I can be of service and contribute to the world in a positive way, and this will help me stay sober."

"The Sudanese—you mean us?" Ahmed pointed to himself. He was still struggling with his addiction to glue, but the boys had decided to let him stay anyway.

I placed my hands on his shoulders and shook him playfully. "Especially you, Ahmed."

I knew another *haboob* would come, and in time, the paint would fade. I hoped the boys would always remember the message, though: they mattered to our world. No matter how irrelevant they thought they were or how irrelevant they appeared to others with their brick-throwing, cat-calling, and glue-sniffing ways, they had the capacity to make a difference in the lives of others just as they'd made a difference in mine.

The same goes for my friends around the world who are addicted and struggling: No matter where you are at in your process whether it be homeless, incarcerated or relapsing again for the second or the umpteenth time, you matter to our world. Your struggle has a place. *You* have a place. Don't give up. You're worth the fight.

***

On my last night in Sudan, my generous neighbors, Martha and Bini, prepared a succulent three-course feast. It was my last meal of Sudanese cuisine and I savored it. We ate it on the roof of our complex beneath a dimly lit half-moon and smoked *tofa*-flavored *sheesha* until our heads hurt. After we gobbled up the last bite, we wished one another well and patted dry kisses onto each other's cheeks.

When they were gone, I peered over the roof's edge and down at the street below. I had dubbed it Peeing Lane because the homeless used it as a public restroom. The scene was pretty revolting and the street smelled, well, like a toilet. But that night, I thought it was the most exquisite thing I'd ever seen. I adored it *for* its irreverence, not in spite of it. Sudan's striking contrasts—atrocious hostilities and extraordinary peace-making—were the contrasts inside *me*.

I began to wonder if I'd made a mistake. Perhaps I should stay one more year. My last days in Sudan weren't looking the way I'd planned *at all*. Where was my sobriety? I felt farther away from it now than when I first arrived, considering that all I could think of these days was several shots of vodka straight-up and warm.

How could I know, standing on the roof that night, what would happen down the line? How could I know that this journey never truly ends? Nearly ten years have passed since I left Sudan. I'll be turning thirty-six soon. In fact, I'm sitting in Utah in my bathtub. (Hey, it's where I do my best writing and reflecting!) Beside me are my two cats, Giz and Tigs, who rest on my makeshift bathtub desk (a chest with a blanket draped over the top) and keep jumping all over my keyboard, and just like Fred cause frantic use of the undo button.

As I sit here soaking in lavender oil and the ease of Sunday morning, I reflect fondly on the irreverent way I left Khartoum. I was, in every sense, a heartbroken girl fleeing in a panic, and due to my PTSD I was headed for the super-nova of downward spirals. According to Hollywood—and its promise of a cookie cutter ending—I had failed the quest.

It wasn't until rewriting this story after I had nearly four years of consecutive recovery time under my belt that I saw the beauty in the *true story*, the one about struggle and darkness, the story that told of a real person on a real mission to find inner peace. This type of expedition is mainly foul and insufferable, but at least it gets your blood pumping and heart racing. Today I know that asking questions and not fitting in doesn't make me rebellious or a bad person; it makes me a soul who was born to break the mold and to challenge what *is*. Sudan, with all its harrowing experiences, helped mold me into a talented and strategic writer, and now I utilize this skill to spread the message of hope to those seeking for recovery from addiction, too.

But I only obtained this clarity *after* immense suffering. When I first landed a contract for this book I was still a punk kid, a real royal egomaniac. The first draft of the story, as my agent, Carolyn, told me, was filled with anecdotes, but lacked depth of character. Carolyn was, in her roundabout way, saying that in my current state of active addiction, *I* lacked depth of character. Of course, as an alcoholic, I was *sure* she was wrong and I was right, and so I pressed on writing and drinking the night away. What happened afterward—the multiple DUIs, the loss of my dream job and book contract, the four years of court-ordered probation—led to experiences of incredible humiliation, rejection, and despair. At rock bottom, I nearly lost my life several nights while drunk driving (and could've harmed another). Fewer than five years ago, I was in a maroon jumpsuit in the Salt Lake County Jail with very little hope of ever making it this far.

At the time I couldn't see it, but my fall from grace was a gift. Ultimately, the suffering led to the obliteration of my ego, that mask we all wear to appear tough and unbreakable but really serves to hide our insecurities and suffocate the budding potential within.

Suffering was the conduit that led to the inner peace I'd been searching for all my life.

I'm still Indy—intent on taking out the bad guy—but instead of focusing my efforts on the hoodlums of the external world, I focus on the only one I'm responsible for: *my ego*. The good news is that the hooligan within is less lethal, and knowing that my dark side is the catalyst to unleashing my great potential allows me to enjoy the experience of being an imperfect human in this rowdy, haphazard world. Hostility and peace-making—these are the contrasts inside all of us. The true battle of good versus evil does indeed lie within. As warriors on Earth we're here only to conquer our own perceptions so that they are beacons of love and compassion for *everyone*. In our own way we are all ships battling the harsh and lonely waters of life, desperate for a space to rest our weary heads and experience peace. By transforming our perceptions from judgement to love we transcend ourselves and heal the planet. This is our great work.

And so, my friends, let us heed the call.

"Shannon! *Numshee!*" Luke called up to me atop the apartment roof.

The cab was here. It was time to go. In fact, I was late.

*"Degiga!"* I called down to him.

Sighing, I hurried down to my apartment, grabbed my bags, and as I whirled around to give my apartment one last look, the zipper to my larger suitcase burst at the seams and spilled out its guts all over the floor.

"Oh come on! *Really?*" I whined, sounding like my dad does when he's been in a traffic jam for too long.

I didn't have a minute or a suitcase to spare so I had to decide quickly what to take and what to leave behind. I threw out clothes I'd brought over from America and stuffed in a beautiful black *jellabiya* I'd found for cheap at the Omdurman *suk*. I packed the goodbye letters that my BES and Unity students had written me and my journals and photos of the people and places I hoped to never forget. Lugging my one suitcase down the stairs, I booked it toward the gate.

"You said I could have your mobile phone when you left?" Luke called after me.

"Luke, the phone. Yes! I'm sorry, but I lost it in the Nile." I'd gone on a canoe ride and the boat had actually flipped over. Thank God I never got bilharziah like the travel doctor said I would. "My apartment is full of stuff—please take whatever you want." I bolted through the gate and toward the cab. The door clanked noisily behind me.

*"Ma'a salama saldig! Ashuuf kum insha'Allah,"* he called after me. I opened the gate and poked my head through.

"Luke, I love you! Don't forget me, okay?"

Moments later I was in the cab cruising past Peeing Lane and then down the streets laid out like a union jack toward Africa Road where Addy and I used to run. We cruised past the buildings that had been damaged in the Garang riots; they were now repaired.

A while later, I was inside the Khartoum National Airport making my way beneath the barely moving fan and over to the men in *jellabiyas* and *turbans*, and the women dressed in sparkly, bright *tobes* sitting at a cut-rate table.

Once on the plane, I collapsed into my seat, my heart playing leap-frog in my chest. The moment felt so final. I closed my eyes and tried breathing into it. I didn't know what the purpose of everything was, but I hoped one day it would become apparent to me. Feeling overwhelmed with gratitude, I closed my eyes and whispered—not to the Mormon God or the Muslim God but to the higher power that made sense to *me:*

"Thank you for the journey."

Not wanting to fly away without one last look at Khartoum I opened my eyes and peered out the window, but, ironically, all I saw was dust.

# Epilogue

*Journal Entry*
*July 12<sup>th</sup>, 2015*

Today is a big day! I've officially completed this book, which, let's face it, has been a long and arduous task. But today I can say that it was all worth it. My life has come full circle. I'm working as the Development and Communications Director for USARA, Utah's Statewide Addiction Recovery Community Organization. USARA's mission is to celebrate, advocate, support, and educate on behalf of drug and/or alcohol addiction recovery and Utah's recovery community. In my position, I develop grant proposals to support innovative peer recovery support services that allow people with a history of addiction—who are currently in recovery—to utilize their lived experience in a professional capacity in order to help others find recovery for themselves. I also use writing to celebrate the milestones of individuals in our recovery community on various platforms, including social media, to offset the sensational and demeaning portrayals in the mass media of people caught in addiction's downward spiral and continue to feed the public's morbid fascination with the dysfunctional side of what is a *preventable and treatable health condition.*

This month, I'll get to present for ARCO's Leadership Academy (ARCO is the Association of Recovery Community Organizations at Faces & Voices of Recovery, and supports the growing network of Recovery Community Organizations (RCOs) throughout the U.S.) My presentation is *Social Media—A Tool for Advocacy and Celebrating Recovery Community*.

Also this month, I'll get to accept The Joel Hernandez Award in Arlington, Virginia, alongside Mary Jo McMillen, USARA's Executive Director (and a courageous advocate, leader, mentor, and friend). This award is being given to USARA by America Honors Recovery, the addiction recovery community's annual awards event to recognize the over 23.5 million Americans in recovery. The Joel Hernandez award recognizes one RCO throughout the U.S. for its success in carrying out a vision and mission of mobilizing the recovery community to increase the awareness, prevalence, and quality of long-term recovery from addiction to alcohol and drugs.

In addition, I'm currently acting as Utah State Captain for UNITE to Face Addiction, a transformative event that will take place in Washington, D.C., on October 4th to ignite and build the National Recovery Movement, a vibrant grassroots recovery advocacy and support movement where courageous individuals in long-term recovery and our allies are uniting for the first time in decades to offer hope and support. As an RCO, USARA is the heart and soul of the recovery movement. In the last ten years, RCOs have multiplied throughout the nation and are representing leadership in their towns, cities, and states, as well as on the national landscape. They have become major hubs for recovery-focused policy advocacy activities, carrying out recovery-focused community education and outreach programs, and are becoming players in system-change initiatives.

The National Recovery Movement is in need of passionate and dedicated recovery leaders to help sustain the recovery movement and drive it forward. Our goal is to challenge deeply rooted social stigmas that have kept recovery voices shrouded in secrecy and shame for far too long.

Personally, I speak out publicly about my struggles in order to shamelessly put a face and voice on addiction and to spread the message that *recovery is possible*. If I can do it, anyone can. I'm asking the public to embrace me as I am: *a human being who's done some really shady things and has some really embarrassing flaws*. Today, I know that flaws don't make me any less worthy of love, compassion, and support, and I hope that by sharing them, I will inspire others to accept and share their own, and in turn set themselves free of the guilt and shame that will end up taking their lives if they're not careful.

By sharing my story, I hope to facilitate a positive conversation around addiction *and* religion in Utah, my home, where a substance use epidemic is wiping out my family, friends, and community members at an alarming rate. Currently, Utah ranks fifth out of all fifty states in the number of opiate-related overdose deaths. This number is higher than the national average and increasing exponentially: in Utah, more people are dying from drug-related deaths than car accidents and firearms.

My desire to self-medicate at an early age stemmed from not being able to choose my own spiritual path while growing up in a Mormon household in Utah's unique religious culture. Utah is the *only* state with a Mormon majority and a majority population belonging to a single church.

As a young person, my desire to seek God differently than the predominant religion caused great heartache. At times, fear-based messaging, manipulation, and control were used to promote religious dogma in an attempt to get me to conform. After years of being bullied and ostracized "in the name of God," I turned to drugs and alcohol in order to cope.

This is not just *my* story but the story of *many*.

Through my work for Utah's addiction recovery community, I've come across so many individuals who are suffering from similar wounds. Our addiction recovery rooms are literally filled with

Mormons and ex-Mormons hiding in shame and secrecy because they've been broken by religious dogma and are afraid to speak out. It's time for our community to address these issues lovingly, compassionately, and in support of our spiritual differences.

In June of this year, I flew to Europe to explore Turkey, Italy, France, and Belgium with my UNFPA friends from New York City. It was the first time I was able to travel internationally since being placed on court-ordered probation after my second DUI in 2009. (Legally, I couldn't leave the state for four years). In Italy, I reconnected with my dear friend William Ezekiel from the *KM* through Facebook. When I saw that he was online, I wrote: *Hi William! Do you remember me?* And he wrote: *Of course I remember you!* Over the years, I've also connected with the Sudanese who are living in Utah, including the Lost Boys who came to Salt Lake City in 2001.

However, it took ten years—that's nearly four thousand days and who knows how many steps—to get here, and at times, I was *absolutely certain* I wasn't going to make it. But I didn't give up. During those terrifying and lonely nights—side effects from using drugs and alcohol for way too long—I clung on to any scrap of hope I could find in the moment, and *eventually* things did fall into place. Yet this only happened after lots of heartache, which today, fortunately, *I can see the value in*. You see, my struggle and this mission have given me a community to belong to. The tough times are easier to handle and absorb if we can remember to take life one day at a time, or as my brave and spirited Sudanese friends say, *shwaya, shwaya*.

# Coming Soon!

## Sex, Drugs & Recovery

## by Shannon Egan

*O*ne year after traveling to Sudan, Shannon hopped on a Greyhound headed for New York City to develop a book regarding her experiences in Africa with well-known literary agency Fifi Oscard. While there, Shannon landed a job writing for the United Nations Population Fund and worked in the Daily News Building in Midtown Manhattan.

To the rest of our world, it appeared Shannon was on top of it. But internally she was a mess. Despite her successes, she suffered from past traumas associated with shame, insecurity, and low self-esteem. In order to cope with the fast-paced and demanding lifestyle of NYC, she relapsed—*hard*.

Her addiction got the best of her and she lost everything: the job, the contract, and the big life in New York. In 2009, Shannon ended up in a jail cell in Utah with a felony DUI and the possibility of a one-year sentence hanging over her head.

*Sex, Drugs & Recovery* highlights Shannon's ugly downward spiral into addiction, but most importantly her recovery process and the purpose and meaning she's found in her struggles through her work as the Development Director for USARA, Utah's statewide Recovery Community Organization, and as a Recovery Advocate for the National Recovery Movement.

## Recovery Resources

For more information regarding the National Recovery Movement or for links to recovery recourses in your area please visit my website at:

www.ShannonEgan.com

Made in the USA
San Bernardino, CA
25 January 2016